Bill

· _____ alot

· _____ ued

Yale also

with Hillary

· been caught

up in drama

and scandals

_____

author.

POLITICAL PROFILES
HILLARY CLINTON

Political Profiles
Hillary Clinton

Catherine Wells

MORGAN REYNOLDS
PUBLISHING
Greensboro, North Carolina

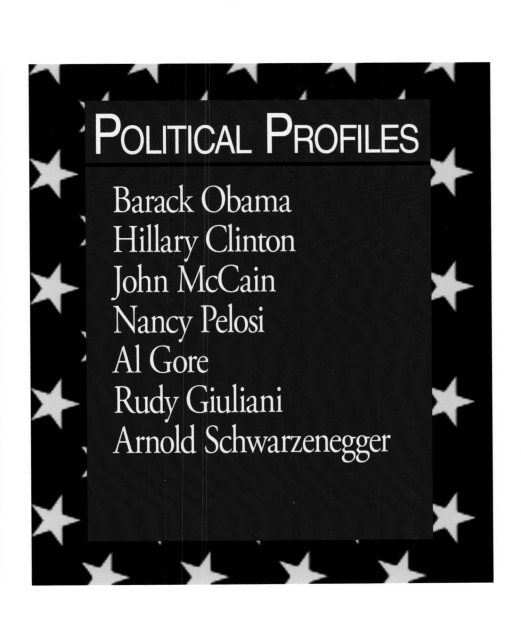

POLITICAL PROFILES

Barack Obama
Hillary Clinton
John McCain
Nancy Pelosi
Al Gore
Rudy Giuliani
Arnold Schwarzenegger

POLITICAL PROFILES: HILLARY CLINTON

Copyright © 2008 by Catherine Wells

Library of Congress Cataloging-in-Publication Data

Wells, Catherine.
   Political profiles : Hillary Clinton / by Catherine Wells.
      p. cm.
   Includes bibliographical references and index.
   ISBN-13: 978-1-59935-047-9
   ISBN-10: 1-59935-047-5
   1. Clinton, Hillary Rodham--Juvenile literature. 2. Presidents' spouses--
United States--Biography--Juvenile literature. 3. Legislators--United States--
Biography--Juvenile literature. 4. Women legislators--United States--Biography-
-Juvenile literature. 5. United States. Congress. Senate--Biography--Juvenile
literature. 6. Presidential candidates--United States--Biography--Juvenile lit-
erature. 7. Women presidential candidates--United States--Biography--Juvenile
literature. I. Title. II. Title: Hillary Clinton.
   E887.C55W45 2007
   973.929092--dc22
   [B]

                         2007028950

Printed in the United States of America
First Edition

6

Contents

Hillary Clinton

one
Park Ridge

On January 20, 2007, a long anticipated video appeared on Hillary Clinton's Web site. In the video, Hillary, who had recently been elected to her second term as senator from New York, announced that she was officially running for president of the United States.

Although the announcement was not a surprise, it was historic nonetheless. Women have run for the highest office in the land before, but none of them was considered to be a significant candidate. The closest a woman had come to the presidency was in 1984, when Democratic candidate Walter Mondale selected Geraldine Ferraro, also from New York, to be his vice-presidential running mate. But the Mondale-Ferraro ticket suffered one of the worst defeats in history.

This time the woman entering the race was one of the strongest candidates. Most polls indicated that Hillary was the strong favorite to secure the nomination of the Democratic Party. The same polls, however, indicated that in a general election, faced off with a Republican nomination, Hillary would have a bigger challenge winning office. Clearly, there are still a large number of voters who are undecided about having a woman as president, but Hillary has more than gender issues to overcome. She and her husband, former president Bill Clinton, are two of the most controversial and polarizing political figures in the U.S. There had been nationwide opposition to her run for the senate from New York; there promises to be even more opposition to her becoming president.

Love her or hate her, no one can deny that Hillary Clinton seems to thrive on challenges. Every step in her career, as a lawyer, parent, wife of a president, and as a politician in her own right, was possible because she had demonstrated commitment and determination. Some of the obstacles that had blocked her way were due to her personal failings, others were created by her enemies and her loved ones, including her husband and political partner.

The life and career of Hillary Clinton is unique in American politics and will certainly be of interest for generations to come—regardless of her success or failure at becoming president.

Hillary has always publicly said that her life has been one of gifts and blessings, regardless of how it looks from the outside. Her parents, who devoted themselves to providing their children with the best possible opportunities in life, were the source of many of these blessings.

Hugh Rodham, Hillary's father, came a long way during his life. He attended Penn State University on a football scholarship, but graduated in the middle of the Great Depression, when millions of people could not find jobs.

Hugh was forced to take a job working in the coal mines of western Pennsylvania before he found better employment as a salesman for Columbia Lace Company, a Chicago drapery manufacturer. There he began a long and successful career, and met his future wife, Dorothy Howell. She was a young secretary from California who applied for a job at Columbia Lace, and quickly hit it off with Hugh. He and Dorothy were married in 1942.

After military service during World War II, Hugh started his own drapery manufacturing business. He worked long hours, and it was not long before he turned the business into a profitable company.

Hillary Diane Rodham, born in Chicago on October 26, 1947, was Hugh and Dorothy's first child. When she was three, the family moved from Chicago to Park Ridge, a suburb north of the city, where Hillary's two brothers, Hugh Jr. and Tony, were born. Although the Rodhams were not wealthy, their new home was large enough to comfortably contain the growing family.

In many ways, the Rodhams were a typical 1950s family. Dorothy worked as a homemaker, while Hugh commuted to Chicago to run the growing drapery business. The family attended a nearby Methodist Church on Sundays, and Hillary and

Hillary as a child
(Courtesy of the National Archives and Records Administration)

her brothers played with other neighborhood children on the peaceful, tree-lined streets.

Hillary soon learned to stand up for herself. Shortly after the Rodhams moved to Park Ridge, a neighborhood girl began picking on the newcomer. Hillary, who had no experience with bullies, began to cry and ran home. Dorothy explained to her daughter that she could either be afraid of the girl and suffer taunts, or stand up to her. "There is no room in this house for cowards," she said.

For a while, Hillary allowed the girl to continue harassing her. Then one day, while the other children looked on, the girl pushed Hillary to the sidewalk and kicked her. After a moment of listening to the laughing onlookers, Hillary stood up and charged at the surprised bully, driving her down the street.

Hugh Rodham Sr., though loving and supportive of his daughter, was a tougher taskmaster than Mrs. Rodham. He believed his children could always achieve more by trying and working harder, and consequently set very high standards, especially in school. If Hillary came home with a good grade he would ask if it was an easy assignment. Hillary worked hard and soon discovered she was a natural leader. She organized games and activities, including a neighborhood circus.

The Rodhams believed strongly in education and wanted the best possible for their children. Dorothy did not have a college degree. Though she enjoyed her life as a home-maker, she sometimes felt uncomfortable talking at social gatherings because of her lack of formal higher education. She wanted more for her daughter; Hillary should never feel inadequate or inferior. The more practical Hugh saw educa-tion as the key to social and financial success. He also made it clear that success and the realization of dreams were not confined to men.

Park Ridge had an excellent public school system. Beginning in elementary school, Hillary made high grades. Reading and writing came easily to her, but she worked even harder on her arithmetic. Outside of school, Hillary participated in Girl Scouts, earning every possible merit badge. She approached each challenge with the same energetic determination.

Sometimes, though, even hard work and determination were not enough. Although Hillary studied piano for years, she was never able to play a melody with more than one hand. She loved dance classes but had little talent for the more difficult ballet stances.

In October 1957, when the Soviet Union launched Sputnik, the first rocket to successfully orbit the earth, Americans became aware of how important science education was to the country's future. During this period, Hillary decided on a career as an astronaut. She wrote a letter to NASA, the agency in charge of America's space program, and requested

After the Soviet Union launched Sputnik in 1957, more emphasis was placed on science education in American schools. *(Courtesy of NASA)*

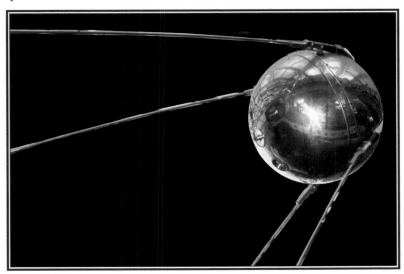

information on preparing for a career in space. But a NASA official wrote back that there was nothing she could do—in that era, women were barred from becoming astronauts. Hillary was angry and disappointed. She was an excellent student, capable of learning the necessary math and science skills. She had never allowed her gender to stop her from achieving her goals, including playing forward on a field hockey team. Now she was being denied an opportunity, not because she was unqualified, but simply because she was a girl.

Later, as she entered Maine East High School, Hillary noticed that many of her girlfriends, who had earned excellent grades in the lower levels, began holding themselves back, attempting to appear less intelligent than they really were. They believed boys would be intimidated by smart girls, and would not ask them out on dates. Other girls took less demanding courses so they could be in the same classes as their boyfriends. Hillary could not understand why her friends would limit themselves in this way.

Although she did not overly concern herself with appearance, Hillary was attractive, with blond hair and bright blue eyes. She was also cheerful, quick to laugh, and eager to be social—but only when she had the time.

Hillary's social life in high school was similar to that of other teenagers all over the country during the early 1960s. She went to school dances and sports events, urging the football and basketball teams toward victory. She spent leisure time hanging out with her friends, drinking cokes or milkshakes. She was part of a large circle of kids from her neighborhood and the adjoining ones. A dozen or so of the group would get together, often at her friend Betsy Johnson's house, where they spent afternoons watching favorite television shows, discussing the latest school gossip or movies and records, and occasionally pigging out on junk food. It was a normal, happy adolescence, occurring before the vast social and cultural changes that would make the late 1960s so turbulent.

Hillary kept busy both in school and out. She organized the school's annual talent shows, and was named head of the committee that arranged and scheduled the student assemblies, which, at a school with an enrollment exceeding 2,500, was a formidable task. As a junior at Maine East High School, she was elected vice president of her class.

Her hard work, first at Maine East, and then during her senior year at Maine South High School, paid off with honors and awards as she neared graduation. At Maine South, she was appointed a senior leader and assisted the faculty with various class instructional duties. Her high grades qualified her to be a member of the National Honor Society, and she won the Good Citizen Award from the Daughters of the American Revolution. To top it off, her senior class voted her as "Most Likely To Succeed."

Hillary's teenage years were not totally devoted to school and extracurricular activities. Her parents also encouraged her to earn her own spending money. She worked part time in a day care center, and baby-sat for younger children in the neighborhood. Later, she worked as a store clerk and had a summer job maintaining the sports equipment in a public park.

Church was important to the Rodham family. They attended the First United Methodist Church every Sunday. The Methodist Church stressed the teachings of founder John Wesley, who believed that it was as important for a

Christian to be as concerned with doing good in the world as she was about her own salvation. Don Jones, fresh out of Drew University, where he had been a student of the progressive-thinking theologian and author Paul Tillich, became a youth minister at First United Methodist. He was to become a strong influence on Hillary and many of her friends, introducing them to new ways of thinking about their social duties as Christians. He used art and popular culture—the socially conscious songs of Bob Dylan, the poetry of e.e. cummings, paintings by Picasso—to introduce his largely upper-middle class students to the world outside affluent Park Ridge.

Reverend Jones helped form many of Hillary's views toward public service and helping the less fortunate. He was also responsible for one of the most exciting events of her adolescence. In 1962, he took his church youth group into Chicago to hear the Reverend Dr. Martin Luther King Jr. give a speech. After the address, Hillary's group was ushered backstage, where Hillary felt honored to shake Dr. King's hand.

In 1962, Hillary attended a speech given by Martin Luther King Jr. Afterward, she was able to meet him and shake his hand. (*Library of Congress*)

The youth group also made trips to the inner city of Chicago, where they helped other organizations working with the urban poor. Hillary even organized a group of volunteers, including several neighborhood boys, who baby-sat for the children of migrant laborers while the parents worked.

Hillary had always considered herself to be a Republican, like her father. In 1964, her senior year of high school, she worked as a "Goldwater Girl," a teenage volunteer on Republican Barry Goldwater's campaign for president. Later, her political affiliation would change, but at the time Hillary was happy to follow her father's lead.

As high school drew to a close, Hillary began thinking of college. She graduated from an excellent high school in the

Hillary's high school senior class portrait *(Courtesy of AP Images)*

top 5 percent of her class and could take her pick of the best universities in the country. Many of her friends chose to attend local schools, such as the University of Chicago, but Hillary wanted to go farther away. She was eager to see the world beyond Park Ridge. After discussing it with her parents, she decided to apply to both Smith and Wellesley. Both were small, prestigious women's colleges; an education at either would prepare her for a successful career in any field she chose.

Both schools accepted her, and she was faced with a difficult decision. Hillary finally decided on Wellesley.

two
Wellesley

Hillary had only seen photographs of Wellesley College before arriving to begin classes, but she was not disappointed. Located on the outskirts of Boston, Massachusetts, Wellesley matched Hillary's ideal of a tradition-steeped institution, with its Gothic stone buildings, tall trees, and well-tended lakes. She soon discovered that many of Wellesley's rules were old-fashioned as well. First-year students could not have a car, entertain boys in their rooms, or leave campus on the weekend without written parental permission. Most social activities consisted of chaperoned dances, afternoon teas, and sporting events.

Some classmates at Wellesley were the daughters of America's most wealthy and influential families. Hillary's best friend throughout college, Eldee Acheson, was the granddaughter of Dean Acheson, President Harry Truman's secretary of state. Another classmate was the daughter of Paul Nitze, deputy secretary of defense in the Kennedy and

Dean Acheson was President Harry Truman's secretary of state. During her time at Wellesley, Hillary became best friends with his granddaughter, Eldee. *(Courtesy of the Lyndon Baines Johnson Library and Museum)*

Johnson administrations and later chief arms negotiator for President Ronald Reagan. This was heady company for a girl from Park Ridge, and years later Hillary admitted to being slightly overwhelmed at first. But she soon overcame her shyness, and her room in Stone-Davis dormitory became the main gathering place for a wide circle of friends.

When she first arrived at Wellesley, Hillary looked much as she had in Park Ridge. Despite her mother's admonitions, she still cared little about her clothes, wore thick glasses, and spent little time styling her hair. Her attire usually consisted of "Peter Pan" blouses and pleated skirts.

However, Hillary's dress soon changed. The thick eyewear gave way to "granny glasses," similar to those made popular by John Lennon, and the skirt-and-blouse outfits were replaced by long peasant dresses or jeans.

Her politics also changed during these years. When Hillary arrived at Wellesley, she believed in the type of individual public service she had learned from her church elders and high school teachers, but thought government action could do little to improve people's lives.

Her experiences at college, both inside and outside the classroom, quickly altered her political philosophy toward more liberal ideas.

Hillary majored in political science. The professor who most influenced her was Alan Schechter, who taught constitutional law. Schechter's main interest was civil rights, which he saw as a moral, as well as a political, issue. Schechter knew most of his students had come from privileged, secure backgrounds, and he attempted to make them aware of how less fortunate people lived. In many ways, Professor Schechter assumed the mentor role toward Hillary that Reverend Jones had served in Park Ridge.

Much of the change in Hillary's political views would result from events occurring in the United States during her time in college. Her four years at Wellesley, 1965-69, were among the most turbulent in American history. The

Vietnam War protesters are being held back by military police in this 1967 photo. *(Courtesy of the National Archives and Records Administration)*

Vietnam War escalated, and increasing numbers of people publicly opposed the conflict. In January of 1968, the North Vietnamese launched a strike deep into South Vietnam that became known as the Tet offensive, and American television networks carried live images of the United States Embassy in Saigon, coming under fierce attack. In April of 1968, Martin Luther King Jr. was killed in Memphis, Tennessee, an event that sparked widespread riots and racial turmoil. Then, on June 5, 1968, Senator Robert Kennedy was assassinated in Los Angeles while campaigning for the Democratic Party's presidential nomination. When the Democratic Convention met in Chicago later that summer to nominate Hubert Humphrey for president, the streets outside the convention hall were alive with protesters. Chicago police used brutal tactics to control the demonstrators, most of whom were young college students.

During this period, many Americans changed their attitudes toward the role of government in America, and toward the nature of society in general. This change was most obvious on college campuses. Students organized antiwar protests. Black students demanded equal opportunities for education, jobs, and housing. And, especially at schools like Wellesley, women began asking why historically they had been denied leadership roles in much of American life.

As the youth movements continued, drugs became more common, and many young people were swept up in their destructive allure. For example, one student who had been voted "Most Likely To Succeed" at Maine East High School died of a drug overdose in 1969.

But Hillary flourished in the way people who had known her in Park Ridge would have expected. Students were attracted by her sense of humor, her friendliness, and her ability to make everyone feel valuable.

Hillary and her friends were concerned with the political and social issues of the day. They agreed that American society and its political parties should better reflect the changes going on around them. But they were not radicals, wishing to tear down the existing social order. Instead, they discussed ways to make government more responsive to people's needs.

Hillary wanted to test her knowledge and ideas against the reality of the world around her. As her understanding increased of how people outside of the suburbs lived, and as she became more knowledgeable about controversial issues, she became less conservative politically. She no longer believed poverty could be ended without government help, or that women and minorities would be treated equally until further laws against discrimination were enacted, and she became convinced that the U.S. should withdraw from Vietnam. She was no longer the "Goldwater Girl" who had first arrived at Wellesley.

However, Hillary never lost confidence in the American system of government. Unlike more militant students, she did not advocate violent revolution or radical change. Hillary's political beliefs changed from the conventional Republican ideas of her father to the Democratic ideas reflected in her friend Eldee Acheson. She also held onto the faith and patriotism that had been important to her as a child.

Hillary maintained a busy schedule during her four years at Wellesley. She volunteered to work in Roxbury, a Boston inner-city neighborhood, as a reading tutor. She also participated in student government.

Hillary also demonstrated her skill as a mediator in a dramatic way. When African American students became convinced that Wellesley was using a secret quota system to keep black enrollment down, they threatened a student strike. Hillary led the effort to reach an agreement between the administration and the black students. She moderated a meeting held in the campus chapel, and made sure both sides in the developing conflict got a fair hearing. Eventually, an agreement was reached, and the student strike was avoided.

In 1968, Hillary showed her increased political consciousness by working as a volunteer on Minnesota senator Eugene McCarthy's campaign for the Democratic presidential nomination. When McCarthy, who campaigned on a platform to end the war, lost the nomination to Hubert Humphrey, Hillary and her friend Eldee Acheson continued to support the Democrats over the Republicans, who nominated Richard Nixon. In the general election campaign, the pair called voters and distributed Humphrey campaign literature. Although Humphrey lost the race in one of the closest elections in history, Hillary enjoyed her first taste of electoral politics.

Hillary's senior year was the culmination of a highly successful college career. She served as president of the student government and used her post to organize a campus wide teach-in about the war in Vietnam. She participated on the nationwide television show *College Bowl*, a popular show of the era that pitted teams from different colleges in quiz competitions. The teams were composed of four players, and the emphasis was on answering highly detailed questions, drawn from several academic disciplines, in a short amount of time. The Wellesley team won multiple rounds, largely due to Hillary's participation, and her success brought her a great deal of publicity. Her senior thesis, entitled "Aspects of the War on Poverty," earned a perfect score, and guaranteed she would graduate with honors. As commencement day approached, Hillary was one of the most respected students on campus.

Several of the students of Hillary's class of 1969 decided that, for the first time ever, a graduating student should be allowed to speak at the commencement ceremony. This was an attitude characteristic of the time, when students all over the country were impatient to be heard. But for conservative Wellesley it was a radical idea, and the college president, Ruth Adams, refused the students' request.

The young women, including Hillary, were not to be deterred. When the student government, and the entire student body, let it be known they supported the idea, the group began deciding on a speaker. If they could approach the president with the name of a highly respected student, someone trusted by both the students and the administration, they were more likely to receive approval.

Hillary was their first choice for speaker, and she accepted the honor. When the students re-approached the college president with their suggestion, Adams agreed—with conditions. The speech could not be embarrassing, or reflect badly on the school. Also, it should not be Hillary's personal speech but should attempt to speak to the entire class.

A team of students worked on the speech for days. They wanted it to summarize their last four years, while voicing their dream and aspirations for the future. When the team finished its work, Hillary added her comments.

The guest speaker for the 1969 Wellesley commencement was Massachusetts senator Edward Brooke. Brooke, a Republican, was the first African American senator since Reconstruction, the era immediately following the Civil War.

Senator Brooke spoke first. Most present that day remember little about his speech except that it was vague, clearly not a speech to satisfy the impatient, activist students of the Wellesley class of 1969.

After the polite applause that followed the senator's words, Hillary approached the podium. She looked small in her bulky black gown and wide mortar board— until she began speaking. "I find myself in a familiar position," she began, "that of reacting, something that our generation has been doing for quite a while now."

Much to the audience's surprise, Hillary diverted from the prepared text. "I find myself

Hillary talks about her Wellesley commencement speech in this photo that appeared in *Life* magazine. *(Courtesy of Lee Balterman/Time Life Pictures/ Getty Images)*

reacting just briefly to some of the things that Senator Brooke said. This has to be brief because I do have a little speech to give," she continued. She went on to say that the senator's remarks reflected what was wrong with his generation. Her generation wanted relevancy, a politics of the impossible made possible. Senator Brooke, and others like him, offered only empathy, and empathy doesn't do us anything. "We've had lots of empathy; we've had lots of sympathy." After criticizing Senator Brooke, Hillary launched into the long speech she and the other students had written, but she had already made her impression.

Hillary's address was featured in *Life* magazine, along with a photo of her dressed in brightly striped pants, balloon-sleeved shirt, sandals, and wire framed glasses. Her college experiences had changed her; she was no longer the bobby-socked girl from Park Ridge. It had been an intense four years, but there would be more changes in her future, especially an encounter with a Rhodes Scholar from Arkansas.

three
Law School

As far back as high school, Hillary's friends had believed her interests in government and public policy would lead her to attend law school. Her ambition had remained steadfast while at Wellesley, where her academic success allowed her to choose from the nation's best law schools.

She quickly narrowed her choices to Harvard and Yale universities. Both contained top law schools. She made her final decision only when a friend, who wanted her to choose Harvard, introduced her to a law professor from that institution. Hillary began questioning him about the school. When the professor interrupted her and said Harvard did not need any more women, Hillary decided to go to Yale.

Yale University, located in New Haven, Connecticut, is one of the most prestigious schools in the country, and counts among its alumni many of the country's past and present leaders. A law degree from Yale would be a great advantage to any career Hillary chose.

The heated politics of the 1960s continued during Hillary's years at Yale. New Haven, home of one of America's premier universities, is also an industrial city with great ethnic diversity. Shortly after Hillary arrived, a politically controversial trial began in a courthouse near the campus. The trial involved the murder trial of Erica Huggins and Bobby Seale, two leaders of the Black Panther Party, a radical black power group that rose to prominence in the 1960s after the death of Malcolm X and the Watts riots in California. Many Black Panther supporters believed the two were arrested on false charges because they were leaders of the militant group. Tensions ran high, and the conflict spilled over onto the Yale campus, where a suspicious fire broke out in the law library, and a student demonstration had to be broken up by police

The Sterling Law Building at Yale University

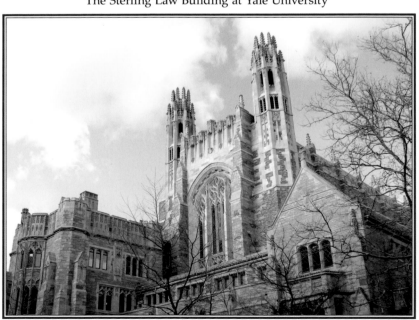

with tear gas. A group of law students demanded their fellow students hold a strike or even seize physical control of the law school. Hillary did not want the school to be closed and was determined to do what she could to keep that from happening.

As angry student activists filled an auditorium and began making rousing speeches to the crowd, Hillary sat quietly on the stage and listened intently to what was said. At the completion of each speech, Hillary asked the speaker questions, to make sure everyone understood what had been said. As the speeches continued, Hillary led the group in discussing ways they could make their unhappiness with the Yale administrators known without closing the law school.

It was also during her first year that Hillary decided on the direction she wanted her law career to take. One day, while reading the notices on a bulletin board, she saw an announcement for an upcoming speech by Marian Wright Edelman. Marian was the wife of Peter Edelman, the director of a League of Women Voters conference Hillary had attended the previous summer. Hillary attended the talk, where Marian spoke about her work in the area of children's rights. Hillary was intrigued by the ideas put forth. After the speech, she asked Marian Edelman if she could work with her in Washington, D.C., during the summer, and Marian agreed.

Hillary spent the next summer working on Capitol Hill, where as part of her job, she interviewed working parents and their children. This experience convinced her that there was a great deal that could be done to improve the lives of America's children. Hillary, who had organized a baby-sitting service for migrant workers' children back in high school, decided to devote her law career to improving children's lives.

Hillary became interested in children's rights after listening to a speech by Marian Wright Edelman. *(Courtesy of AP Images)*

When she returned to Yale for her second year, she began taking courses on children and the law. She also worked at the Yale Child Studies Center and later collaborated with two professors on books about the role of children in the legal and educational systems.

Hillary's reputation among her fellow law students grew quickly. She was a formidable presence, someone who was highly intelligent, disciplined, and destined for success. There was another student who had a similar reputation for high achievement: Bill Clinton. He was older than most of the other students, because he had spent two years studying in Oxford, England, as a Rhodes Scholar. The Rhodes Scholarship, the world's oldest international fellowship, is considered one of the highest honors that can be given to a graduating college senior. But Bill, besides being well educated, was tall, charming, and an engaging conversationalist.

Bill quickly became popular at Yale. Most of the people who met him almost instantly understood that he wanted a career in politics—and would be good at it.

Hillary and Bill saw one another around campus several times before they were introduced. Once they had been introduced they almost immediately began dating.

Although Hillary and Bill were similar in many ways, their respective childhoods had taken somewhat different paths. When Bill was born, on August 19, 1946, his mother was already a widow. Bill's father, William Jefferson Blythe III, died in a car wreck four months before Bill was born. As a young child, Bill lived with his maternal grandparents in Hope, Arkansas, while his mother studied nursing in New Orleans. He loved his grandparents, but the separation from his mother was painful.

When Bill was four, his mother returned to Hope and married a car dealer, Roger Clinton. Later, the family moved to Hot Springs, Arkansas, where Bill's younger brother, Roger Jr., was born. Roger Clinton Sr. later adopted Bill, and he changed his name to William Jefferson Clinton.

Life in the Clinton house was not always pleasant. Roger Clinton was an alcoholic and often became abusive. Bill witnessed drunken rages, including physical attacks on his mother. However, even with these problems, Bill graduated at the top of his high-school class and won a partial scholarship to Georgetown University in Washington, D.C. While at Georgetown, Bill earned excellent grades, worked part-time in Arkansas senator William Fulbright's Capitol Hill office, and participated in student politics. His time at Georgetown was as active as Hillary's years at Wellesley.

As graduation approached, Bill was awarded the Rhodes Scholarship. While at Oxford, Bill studied government and philosophy, and traveled around Europe. After two years at Oxford, Bill accepted a scholarship to study law at Yale.

Bill did not live in a dormitory at Yale but shared a house with three other students at nearby Fort Trumball Beach. Hillary soon became a regular guest. The friends played volleyball on the beach and shared potluck dinners; evenings were often spent discussing the issues of the day.

Hillary and Bill seemed made for each other. But, as Bill admitted later, he worried about becoming romantically involved with Hillary because of their different career plans. He was determined to return home and pursue a political career. Hillary knew little about Arkansas, but it was not where she had planned to live. Her plans centered on either Washington, D.C., or New York City. Arkansas seemed like a place near the end of the earth.

The young couple did not let the future distract them too much, however. They competed as a team in a mock trial, held to help train law students to argue cases before a judge and jury. Although they approached the project with their typical zest and determination, they failed to win the competition. Bill joked they lost because Hillary wore a bright red dress which distracted the judge's attention.

In the fall of 1972, the couple took time away from classes to travel to Texas to work for the campaign of George McGovern, the Democratic nominee for president. McGovern's chief issue was ending the Vietnam War, and he won the support of millions of young people tired of the long conflict. Both Bill and Hillary were enthusiastic McGovern supporters. Hillary registered voters near the Texas-Mexico border, and

Bill Clinton (left) walks beside George McGovern (center) and Joe Purcell. In 1972, Bill and Hillary worked for McGovern's presidential campaign. *(Courtesy of AP Images)*

Bill worked in the Austin headquarters. Although McGovern lost in a landslide to Richard Nixon in the November election, Hillary made several close friends during the campaign. One was Betsey Wright, who would later work for Bill when he became governor of Arkansas.

Bill visited Hillary's parents over the Christmas break of 1972. At first, the Rodham family was unsure what they thought about the extroverted young man from Arkansas. But before the week was out, they had been charmed by his warmth and enthusiasm. However, the Rodhams did not want Hillary to move to Arkansas. In the spring, Hillary paid a visit to Bill's family. She later admitted that before the visit she had believed the state was populated by hillbillies spitting tobacco juice out of pickup trucks. Instead, she discovered it was a beautiful state and that the people were warm and friendly. However, she still did not want to live in a rural Southern state.

Back at Yale, Hillary did not allow her romance with Bill to distract her from her studies. She remained at the top of her class. Her interest in children and the law continued, and she decided to stay at Yale an extra year to continue work at the Yale Child Study Center. There, she studied child development, extending her expertise in children's legal rights in the context of how children develop emotionally and intellectually. She worked in the nursery, analyzed language development, assisted with diagnostic tests, and studied children's literature, and collaborated on a book, *Beyond the Best Interests of the Child*, which proposed methods the courts could use to insure that custody decisions were in the child's best interest.

As graduation approached for the couple, the question of whether to continue their romance remained unsolved. Bill never wavered from his determination to return to Arkansas, and Hillary still felt she needed to pursue a law career in one of the larger cities. It was an agonizing period for both young people.

In the spring of 1973, Bill left for Arkansas. Hillary decided to move to Cambridge, Massachusetts, to work with Marian Wright Edelman in her new organization, the Children's Defense Fund.

four
Young Lawyer

*H*illary had wanted to work for the Children's Defense Fund since first meeting Edelman three years before. Edelman began her career as an attorney for the NAACP, the pioneer civil rights organization. She founded the Children's Defense Fund "to create a viable, long-range institution to bring about reforms for children."

One of the organization's primary goals was to fully implement the Head Start program. Head Start provided poor preschool children the medicine, nutrition, and guidance necessary to succeed in school. Although the program, founded in the late 1960s, has generally been considered a success, even by most critics of social programs, it has never been fully funded by the federal government. For example, in 1988 only 16 percent of eligible children participated in the program.

From its beginning, the Children's Defense Fund has been controversial. Some critics view it as a pressure group

Marian Wright Edelman sits in front of a Children's Defense Fund banner. Hillary worked as a staff attorney for the Children's Defense Fund after graduating from Yale. *(Courtesy of AP Images/Dennis Cook)*

advocating wasteful government spending; others are wary of any group that argues for a larger federal role in children's lives. They fear that the right of the parents to raise their children as they think best is put to risk when the government becomes too deeply involved in a family's decisions.

At the Children's Defense Fund, Hillary worked as a staff attorney, responsible for researching ways to change laws protecting children. However, Hillary was not to stay long at the Children's Defense Fund.

1973 was another critical year in U.S. history. The last U.S. soldiers came home from Vietnam. The Supreme Court handed down the *Roe v. Wade* decision, which precluded states from passing law outlawing abortion—and the Watergate scandal threatened the presidency of Richard Nixon. Watergate involved a series of crimes committed by President

Nixon's 1972 reelection campaign workers. The most famous incident was a break-in at the Democratic Party's National Headquarters in a Washington, D.C., office building called The Watergate.

As 1973 drew to a close, the nation's attention was riveted on a Congressional investigation of the scandal. In January of that year, Hillary received a call from John Doar, a lawyer working with the House Judiciary Committee, which was investigating President Nixon's role in trying to hide his campaign's involvement in the Watergate burglaries. Doar asked Hillary to come work on his staff. Although Hillary loved her work with the Children's Defense Fund, an offer to work in Washington was too good to turn down.

Hillary's work involved researching legal procedures. She spent long hours reading law books and writing guidelines for the committee to follow. But as it became evident that

Hillary (center) stands beside John Doar (left) in the Judiciary Committee hearing room as impeachment charges are brought against President Richard Nixon. *(David Hume Kennerly/Getty Images)*

President Nixon was involved in the scandal, Hillary realized she was a participant in a historical series of events.

As the Watergate investigation developed, a series of recorded conversations between President Nixon and his top aides became the central issue. Nixon had earlier installed a recording system in his office. The House Judiciary Committee demanded to hear certain tapes on which they believed the Watergate break-in was discussed by the president and his aides. When Nixon refused to turn over the tapes, the Judiciary Committee took its plea to the Supreme Court, where finally the White House was ordered to release the tapes.

One of Hillary's assignments was to listen to the White House tapes. She spent many hours locked in a small office, with an armed guard outside the door, listening to and transcribing the conversations between President Nixon and his aides as they discussed ways to keep the American people from discovering the truth about the Watergate break-in. The tapes eventually provided the evidence that forced Richard Nixon to resign his office, and Hillary was one of the first Americans to hear them.

Her experience with the House Judiciary Committee deepened Hillary's interest in politics. Children's issues were still a primary concern, but the process of watching government up close during this dramatic period strengthened her conviction that young, idealistic people should become involved in public affairs.

While in Washington, Hillary shared a house with Sarah Ehrman, an old friend from the McGovern campaign. She also met several influential people who were impressed by the young lawyer; she took time out from her busy schedule for job interviews with some prestigious Washington law firms.

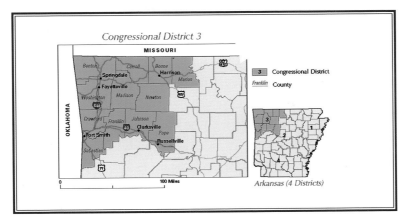

Shortly after Hillary moved to Arkansas, Bill began a campaign to win the congressional seat for the Third District in Arkansas. *(Courtesy of the National Atlas)*

Almost without exception the interviewers were impressed and wanted her to join their firms. Hillary had other choices; she could establish herself as a prominent Washington attorney, or return to the Children's Defense Fund.

There was still the matter of Bill Clinton, now teaching at the University of Arkansas Law School, and preparing to run for congress from the Third Congressional District in his home state. They had stayed in touch by phone and through letters; now Hillary decided to pay him a visit. She traveled to Fayetteville, where the University of Arkansas is located. She thought the town was lovely. Bill introduced her to Wylie Davis, dean of the law school, who asked her to apply for a job teaching at the law school. She thanked him for the offer, but said she was still undecided about the next step in her career.

Hillary returned to Washington and reconsidered the job offers from the Washington law firms. She knew such employment would involve years of hard work but the

The Old Main building at the University of Arkansas. Hillary accepted a teaching position at the university to be with Bill, who also taught there. *(Photo by Christopher Ott)*

financial rewards, and her ability to impact the issues she cared about, would be great. But Bill was in Arkansas. After a few days of consideration, she called Davis and told him she would take the teaching job.

She asked her friend and colleague Sarah Ehrman, who was also her landlady in Washington, to drive her to Arkansas. Sarah agreed, but only because it would give her time to talk Hillary out of the move, which many of her friends considered a disastrous decision. During the two-day drive to Fayetteville, Sarah asked repeatedly: "Why are you doing this? Are you crazy? Why are you going to this rural place? You could have a fabulous job. You could fight for what you believe in."

Sarah even tried to get Hillary to convince Bill to move to Washington. "He could teach at Georgetown," she told Hillary. "He could do anything he wanted to do, he's so smart, why?

But it was no use. Hillary had made up her mind. "I love him," she told Sarah. "I want to be with him."

Hillary arrived in Fayetteville in August, and quickly began preparing for her first year as a law professor. She was assigned to teach criminal law, civil procedure, and children's law. But she also explored her new home and soon decided that she was going to be happy in the small town atmosphere. In some ways, Fayetteville reminded her of Park Ridge. The people were friendly and helpful, and had many of the same values.

When Hillary arrived, Bill was in the middle of his first political campaign. He was running against John Paul Hammerschmidt, a popular Republican incumbent. Few people expected him to win, but he was gaining attention as an intelligent, attractive young candidate. The campaign needed Hillary's help, though. Bill was charismatic, dedicated, and hardworking—but his campaign style was haphazard. He would return to his Fayetteville home after a day of meeting voters with the names of important contacts falling from his pockets. His volunteer campaign workers complained about the chaos. With her usual energy and efficiency, Hillary began organizing his campaign. She assigned people specific tasks, arranged Bill's schedule, and helped to write and edit his speeches.

Hillary even invited her family down to help with Bill's campaign. Although the Rodhams still had doubts about Hillary moving permanently to Arkansas, they supported her decision. Even Hugh Sr., a lifelong Republican, agreed to interrupt his retirement to come to Arkansas and help.

Bill's campaign quickly improved, and some observers began to say he might win. But the incumbent was too well entrenched. Bill lost the race but did receive a higher percentage of votes than any previous challenger.

After the campaign, Hillary's mother and father returned to Park Ridge. But her brothers enjoyed Fayetteville and decided to stay and take classes at the university.

During the campaign, Hillary had traveled the twenty-four counties that comprised the Third District, and she was impressed by the state's beauty. She also liked the fact that everyone seemed to know each other, and loved the warm, southern graciousness, and deep concern for family she found in the small towns. And her experiences at the law school were positive. In a short time, Hillary felt at home in Arkansas.

One day Hillary was concerned about a student who had not been in class. When she called information and requested the student's number, the operator, instead of looking up the number, simply told her the student was not at home. The young man had gone camping, the operator said. Hillary hung up the phone, shaking her head. The operator knew the person she was trying to contact. This was a long way from impersonal, anonymous Washington, D.C.

After the campaign, Hillary and Bill enjoyed working as colleagues on the law school faculty. Bill was known as an easygoing teacher. Hillary, however, was considered a hard taskmaster who demanded the most from her students.

Much as they had at Yale, Hillary and Bill quickly gathered a large group of friends. They had dinner parties, went to football games, and played volleyball and cards. One thing Hillary discovered about Bill was his competitive nature. He loved to win at everything he did.

As much as she liked Arkansas, Hillary still wondered if

she had made a mistake by leaving Washington. After her first year of teaching, she decided to take a trip north to visit old friends. Bill stayed behind in Fayetteville, but he drove her to the airport and on the way, they passed a red brick house, which was for sale. Hillary described the house as "sweet-looking."

When Hillary returned from her trip, she was committed to spending her life with Bill. On the ride from the airport, he reminded her of the little red house. "I bought it," he said, "so now you'd better marry me because I can't live in it by myself."

Two months later the couple married, on October 11, 1975. The affair was a small, private ceremony. Invited guests included family and friends from Yale and the law school faculty. Roger Clinton Jr., Bill's half brother, acted as best man. Hillary chose to keep her maiden name, Rodham. After the wedding reception, Bill and Hillary, along with the entire Rodham family, left for a honeymoon in Acapulco.

Hillary Rodham had decided to abandon a successful career as a Washington lawyer and move to Arkansas in order to marry the man she loved. It was a decision that infuriated some of her friends. They believed she was making the same mistake she had warned others against back at Maine East High School—relinquishing a cherished goal for a man. Hillary did not attempt to rebut their criticisms. She had done what she thought was right. She had joined her future with Bill Clinton's, for better or for worse.

five

Victory and Defeat

After their honeymoon, Hillary and Bill returned to teaching at the law school. But they both hoped they would not stay in Fayetteville much longer. Bill had plans on moving to Little Rock, the state capital, as an elected official.

Bill had a conversation with Jim Guy Tucker, the Arkansas attorney general. Tucker told him that he was going to run for Congress, and that Bill should try for the soon-to-be-vacant office of attorney general. Bill began planning a campaign.

In the meantime, Hillary continued to teach classes and to promote community issues of special interest to her. She formed a group committed to reforming the laws covering rape and sexual assault. She also helped start a rape crisis center for victim counseling and won funding from lawyer groups in Arkansas for a legal aid center to provide representation for poor people.

One story from this time reveals Hillary's growing resourcefulness as a lawyer. One day she received a call and was told that a woman who preached on the streets of Fayetteville had been arrested for disturbing the peace. A judge had decided to send the woman to a state mental institution.

The street preacher convinced Hillary she was not crazy, but she steadfastly refused to stop her street preaching. Hillary continued to talk to her, and discovered the woman had family in California. She knew the woman could not remain free in Arkansas, and so suggested to the judge that it would be cheaper to buy a ticket to California than to put the woman in an institution. The judge agreed, and the preacher left for California to continue her religious work.

During these years, Hillary also wrote a series of articles for scholarly journals, such as the *Harvard Educational Review.* The articles advocated a wider range of legal rights for children and argued that in special situations children should have the same constitutional rights as adults. The underlying legal philosophy in the writings is that a child under a specific age, usually eighteen in the United States, should not automatically be considered property of the family, a legal precedent extending back to the eighteenth century. Hillary wrote that children should be evaluated as individuals by the court. If the child is determined to be "competent," a legal term indicating that a person is capable of speaking for him or herself in a court of law, he or she should enjoy the full rights of citizenship.

In her writings, Hillary entered a lively debate about the rights of children in modern society. The articles were written for a relatively small group of intellectuals who study the changing roles of children and families.

Hillary has said many times that she loved teaching and living in Fayetteville. But this happy period was coming to a close. In 1976, Bill was elected as the Arkansas attorney general. This win meant a move to Little Rock, the state capital. In Arkansas, the attorney general, who serves as the state's attorney in court cases and also controls the state police, is the second most powerful state leader.

After Bill was sworn in as attorney general, Hillary began looking for a new job. The Rose Law Firm, the oldest law firm west of the Mississippi River, offered her the chance to become one of the first women in the state hired by a major firm.

Although she performed varied legal tasks, Hillary continued taking children's cases, often without pay. Usually these cases involved conflicts surrounding divorce. Hillary always argued for the best interests of the child.

In 1977, she received a high honor when President Carter appointed her to the national board of directors of the Legal Services Corporation, a federally funded agency that helps poor people in civil cases, such as disputes with landlords. The job involved frequent travel to Washington.

She also started an organization called the Arkansas Advocates for Children and Families. The group studied the problems facing poor children in the state and pressured politicians to fund programs to help them. Hillary served as the group's first president.

Bill's tenure as attorney general was successful. He pushed for stronger ethics laws for politicians and argued that utility companies charged unfair rate increases to Arkansas citizens. He also worked with the state police to bring down the crime rate. Bill was undoubtedly the rising star of Arkansas politics.

It was a busy time for the young couple. But as usual, they found time to make new friends and to stay in touch with old ones. In Little Rock, they bought another small house, where they entertained often. As in law school, conversation at the dinner parties was usually about politics and public policy. But occasionally, Bill played his saxophone for friends, or they listened to records and danced.

As the election year of 1978 approached, Bill decided to run for governor of Arkansas. Although only thirty-two, it was the natural next step for the ambitious attorney general.

However, Hillary and Bill knew a gubernatorial campaign would put them both under intense media scrutiny. In the conservative southern state of Arkansas, a wife with her own career, one who had kept her maiden name after marriage, could certainly be a political detriment.

During the campaign, Hillary was criticized for keeping her maiden name, for having a career outside the home, and for the articles she had written on children's rights. Bill's opponents, in both the Democratic and Republican parties, also hoped that making an issue of Hillary's independence would make Bill appear weak. "If he could not control his wife, how could he control the state?" was their argument.

Bill and Hillary ignored the critics. In his speeches, Bill emphasized improving education and strengthening the state's economy. Hillary continued to perform her role as chief advisor. Bill won the election, capturing more than 60 percent of the vote. When he assumed office in January of 1979, he became the youngest governor in the United States.

However, Bill's first term would be a difficult period. Hillary continued to be criticized by the media. The gown she wore to the inaugural ball was criticized mercilessly.

At that time, the governor of Arkansas served a two-year term. Bill wanted to resolve several severe state problems

Hillary and Bill attend a White House dinner shortly after Bill was elected governor of Arkansas. *(Courtesy of AP Images/Barry Thumma)*

in the first term. He pushed the state legislature to increase spending on education and to merge school districts to create more balanced funding; to reform the method used to increase utility rates; and to raise car licensing fees and use the money to repair the decaying road system.

It was a large agenda, and many Arkansans opposed it and sought ways to undercut it. One tactic was to portray Hillary as a radical feminist and outsider. She was criticized for her dress, for her hair, for working as a lawyer instead of a homemaker. But the keeping of her maiden name after marriage brought on the heaviest attacks. Letters asking, "Don't you love your husband?" and accusing her of being "uppity" were delivered almost daily to the Governor's Mansion.

Hillary did not always help herself. One photograph, published throughout the state, showed the couple at a University of Arkansas football game. While the crowd, including football fan Bill Clinton, cheered and waved their arms, Hillary sat quietly reading a book. Hillary seemed to resent the public relations role the First Lady was expected to play, and this attitude angered some Arkansans.

Bill's popularity began to fade. The hike in car license tag fees was highly controversial. Although the money was to be used to fix roads, the increase angered many automobile owners. Bill had other troubles. His proposal to spend the money on the Arkansas educational system was unpopular with many legislators, and teachers resisted taking a competency test.

But nothing hurt Bill's popularity more than President Carter's decision to house thousands of Cuban refugees, released by dictator Fidel Castro in 1980, at Fort Chaffee,

President Carter and Bill Clinton

Arkansas. The decision was unpopular, and when some detainees escaped in May 1980, state residents were outraged. Then, in June, Fort Chaffee erupted into a riot, and fear spread throughout the state. Bill called out the National Guard and the rioters were stopped, but he was blamed for the violence.

Although 1980 was difficult for Bill's career, one happy event did occur on February 27, when Hillary gave birth to a daughter. The couple had attended natural childbirth classes, but the baby was positioned wrongly in the womb and had to be delivered by Caesarean section. After the delivery, Bill walked the hospital corridors cradling his new daughter in his arms. The couple named their new daughter Chelsea, after "Chelsea Morning," one of their favorite Judy Collins songs.

Bill and Hillary with Chelsea in this 1980 family photo *(Courtesy of AP Images/Donald R. Broyles)*

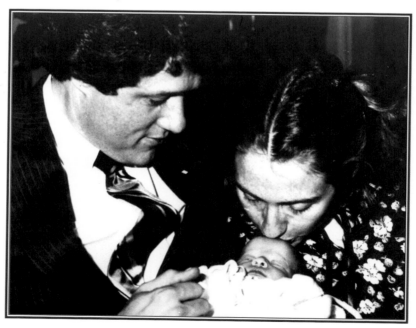

As the 1980 campaign began, it was clear that Bill was in political trouble. President Carter, also a Democrat, was running for reelection, and many Arkansans were still angry with the president for housing the Cubans at Fort Chaffee. Bill's reelection chances suffered as a consequence. His opponent in the campaign, businessman Frank White, ran a series of television commercials linking Bill to the unpopular Carter.

Bill's reelection effort also suffered because Hillary was busy with her job and the new baby, which left her little time to help with campaign strategy.

Frank White won the 1980 gubernatorial race by a slim margin, and Bill became the youngest ex-governor in the United States. It looked as though Bill's bright political star had fallen from the sky.

As the couple packed to move out of the Governor's Mansion, they faced an uncertain future. While Bill's career had come to a halt, Hillary's career was progressing rapidly. Many of their friends worried about the strain on their marriage; clearly the new decade was going to be a stressful time.

six

Ms. Clinton

After leaving the Governor's Mansion, Bill became extremely depressed. Losing the election was a tough blow. At this critical time, Bill's pastor at the Immanuel Baptist Church in Little Rock asked the Clintons to come along on a church-sponsored trip to Israel and the Holy Land. During the tour, Bill seemed to gain new strength, and Hillary was delighted to see his old fighting spirit return.

Back in Arkansas, Bill had to decide his future plans. Hillary suggested that he take a job in a law firm, and he thought the idea a good one. But they both hoped his career as a lawyer would only be temporary; he now planned to regain the governor's office in 1982.

Hillary returned full-time to her busy law practice. After she was made a full partner in the firm, her work load increased. In addition to working on her own cases, she shared responsibility for managerial decisions. The increased responsibility did have one benefit, however. Soon she was earning nearly $400,000 a year, considerably more than the $35,000 Bill had earned as governor.

During these trying years, when her husband was often traveling and her career demanded greater amounts of time, Hillary also had to learn the complicated skills of motherhood. "Chelsea, this is new for both of us," Hillary recalled telling her baby daughter. "I've never been a mother before, and you've never been a baby. We're just going to have to help each other do the best we can."

As the election year of 1982 approached, Hillary needed to make several decisions. She wanted Bill to regain the governorship, but many voters had shown they felt threatened by her. Although she shared many of the core values of Arkansans, such as a strong faith, and devotion to children and family, Bill's political opponents had succeeded in characterizing her as an enemy to those beliefs. She needed to correct this misconception.

Her appearance was part of the problem. The frumpy clothes and frizzy hair had left her open to criticism as a First Lady who did not create a proper image. She replaced the big glasses with contact lenses; had her hair cut and styled; replaced the baggy dresses with smartly tailored suits; and on occasion, wore lipstick and eye shadow, as another bow to fashion.

She decided to campaign as Hillary Clinton, but was quick to point out that Bill had not pressured her to make the change. It was her personal decision.

After she made the changes, Hillary received a great deal of positive press. Many of the same writers and reporters who had previously criticized her now spoke of her in kinder terms.

During Bill's 1982 gubernatorial campaign, Hillary changed her appearance in an attempt to connect with Arkansas voters. (*Courtesy of AP Images*)

But many of her friends were unhappy. Betsey Wright, the Democratic Party activist Hillary and Bill had met in 1972, said, "I teared up. I had a lump in my throat." However, Hillary had made her decision, and despite any personal sadness she may have felt, she campaigned for Bill in her characteristically determined way.

During the campaign, some commentators began speaking of Hillary as a more able politician than Bill. She was seen as the more articulate of the two and quicker to reach decisions. Hillary was suddenly being discussed as a political figure in her own right.

She had a generally positive effect on the campaign. Her changes in name and appearance won support, and she continued to make many strategic campaign decisions. She may have softened her image, but within the campaign she was still the same Hillary, and that meant she could be more exacting than her husband.

Arkansans responded positively to the return of Bill and Hillary. Traveling around the state, Bill and Hillary realized many of the people who had voted against Bill in 1980 had merely wanted to "send him a message" about certain issues but did not really want to replace him as governor. Now they were willing to give him a second chance at running the state.

Frank White campaigned for reelection by using the same strategy that had worked in 1980. He depicted Bill and Hillary as radicals out of touch with the average voter. Bill's speeches, however, stressed the need to improve education and to attract higher paying jobs to the state.

Bill won the 1982 election with 54.7 percent of the vote. His political career was still alive. As the young family returned their belongings to the small living quarters within the Governor's Mansion, Bill knew he owed much of his comeback to the efforts, and personal sacrifices, of Hillary. They were forging the bonds of a political marriage unlike any seen before in American politics.

seven
Arkansas Decade

When he returned to office, Bill's first priority was to improve the state's education system. The schools in Arkansas ranked near the bottom in every national survey, and he knew it was time for improvement.

To accomplish his education goals, Bill needed the legislature to pass a number of reforms. He also knew improvements in education would cost money, and that meant raising taxes. Although Arkansas had the lowest tax rates in the country, raising taxes in the state was difficult—even the suggestion had destroyed several politicians' careers. The people of the state would have to be convinced the measure was absolutely necessary.

Bill decided the best way to make the public aware of what needed to be done was to form a public committee to travel the state and to gather information from local school boards, teachers, and concerned parents. The committee would then formalize the reform recommendations and he would ask the legislature to put them into law. The people selected to sit on the committee would be critical to its success, and Bill labored over the selection process.

But one committee selection was easy. Bill named Hillary to chair the group, though it was politically risky to appoint his wife to such an important post. Announcing Hillary's selection, he said she would "guarantee that I will have a person who is closer to me than anyone else, overseeing a project that is more important than anything else. I don't know if it's politically a wise move, but it's the right thing to do."

Hillary was enthusiastic about the new challenge. The public education she had received in Park Ridge public schools had prepared her for a successful life, and she wanted the children of Arkansas to have the same opportunity. She began traveling the state to solicit suggestions and to gain support for the initiatives.

Hillary gives a speech about early childhood education. *(Courtesy of AP Images/Charles Rex Arbogast)*

Hillary visits with children at a child development center. *(Courtesy of the Department of Defense)*

Hillary's task was helped when, in 1983, the National Commission on Excellence in Education issued a report on the quality of the country's schools. The report, entitled "A Nation At Risk," spoke of a "rising tide of mediocrity" in education, and said that inadequate education was the gravest threat to the country's future success. Suddenly the nation's attention was focused on improving schools, and education reform became one of the hottest political topics in the country. Bill and Hillary found themselves on the leading edge of a national debate.

During her travels around the state, Hillary made certain that the ideas and opinions of local leaders were heard. Often she would begin a meeting with a roomful of people who were opposed to any education reforms that would necessitate higher taxes. But after she made the case that economic growth would not come to the state until the workforce was better educated, most would leave the meeting convinced it was time to sacrifice for their children's future. The committee was soon known as the "Hillary Committee."

When the group's work was finished, it issued a list of recommendations, including mandatory kindergarten, smaller class sizes, longer school years, better school counselors, teacher-competency tests, and more class credits required for high school graduation. Most concerned parents supported the recommendations, but one suggestion created a political firestorm.

The controversy erupted over the so-called "teacher testing" part of the bill. The section required teachers to pass a competency test before they could receive a pay raise. The teachers protested: hundreds announced they would not take the test. The Arkansas Education Association spoke out against the move, and when Bill made it clear that teachers would have to take the test before he asked the legislature to raise taxes, the attacks on Bill and Hillary intensified. One school librarian was quoted as saying the Clintons were "lower than snakes."

Teachers booed Hillary's speeches, and catcalls often met her when she toured a school. Although disappointed in the reaction, she continued her work, refusing to let criticism sway her from what she thought was the right path for the state's students.

The controversy over teacher competency tests brought Bill, and indirectly Hillary, national attention. Newspapers with national circulation, such as the *New York Times* and the *Washington Post*, carried articles about the dispute. Bill was a guest on the CBS Sunday morning news show, *Face*

Hillary served as a paid director on Wal-Mart's corporate board during the 1980s. *(Courtesy of AP Images/April L. Brown)*

for some of the pollution in Arkansas's rivers and streams, Hillary's position on the board of directors raised questions about the close relationship between the governor's wife and the company. Although no one charged that any laws were broken, Hillary's paid position with the company seemed inappropriate to some.

Hillary's life in Arkansas was full and exciting. Chelsea started school, and even with her busy schedule, Hillary tried to spend time with her daughter every day. Hillary or Bill drove Chelsea to school in the morning. When out of town, Hillary made video tapes of herself and left them for her daughter to watch.

Chelsea, an excellent student, skipped a grade in school. She enjoyed sports, and played on softball and soccer teams. She also loved ballet and danced in recitals from an early age. In Little Rock, her parents tried to attend every game, where Bill would sometimes embarrass her by cheering loudly. On weekends and holidays, it was not uncommon to see the family playing softball or touch football on the mansion's lawn.

Another characteristic of the Clintons in Little Rock was their informality. One old friend later told of calling at the mansion one night. Hillary and Bill greeted him and his wife in their bathrobes, and immediately invited them inside to have a late snack in the kitchen.

Much of the family's entertaining took place around the kitchen table. Friends would gather to snack on treats from the refrigerator and play cards and tell stories. Both Clintons were skilled storytellers. Hillary was especially good at retelling episodes from her law practice, including anecdotes about some of the colorful characters from the more rural areas of Arkansas. She often illustrated her stories by pretending to spit tobacco juice from the side of her mouth. Bill, not to be undone, mastered an authentic Arkansas hog call.

The 1980s was a decade of political success for the Clintons. Although his opponents continued to characterize him as a liberal who was out of touch with the average Arkansan, the voters returned Bill to office in 1984, 1986, and 1990. He was always quick to give Hillary much of the credit for his success. There was even talk of Hillary succeeding her husband as governor, including reports that she had asked political supporters if they thought she could win. But Hillary publicly denied any interest in running for governor and stated that she worked best in a supporting role.

By 1988, Bill had a national reputation as a bright, progressive governor, and many pundits thought he would run that year for the Democratic Party's nomination for president of the United States. Bill had never denied that he was interested in being president some day. It had been a dream since he was a boy. But he was not convinced 1988 was the best year for him to run. Chelsea was only seven, and a national campaign would separate her from Hillary and Bill for long periods of time. Although he received promises of support from many Democrats, Bill finally decided not to attempt a campaign in 1988.

However, Bill continued working in national politics, and his reputation continued to grow. He served as chairman of the National Governors Association, and as leader of a group of moderate Democrats called the Democratic Leadership Council. Hillary also traveled nationally, speaking and lecturing about her work in Arkansas, and promoting the Children's Defense Fund.

Life for the family in Arkansas was rich and rewarding. However, it was almost certain that Bill would eventually make a run for the presidency. When that time came, the family would be forced onto the national stage. As the fall presidential campaign between Vice-President George H. W. Bush and Massachusetts governor Michael Dukakis approached, Hillary and Bill thought that they had at least four more years before they would have to contend with the national media. But they were not counting on the publicity that would be generated by a speech Bill was scheduled to give at the 1988 Democratic National Convention.

eight
Campaign Issues

*B*ill was flattered when Michael Dukakis asked him to put his name into nomination at the Democratic National Convention. Dukakis, who was not popular in the south, hoped Bill's nominating speech would win him southern support.

But the speech almost ended Bill's career—and it was Hillary who did the most to salvage it.

Bill usually wrote his own speeches but at the convention the Dukakis campaign staff insisted he read an address they had prepared. Bill's delivery stumbled at the more awkward passages of the poorly written speech. The crowd, impatient for the nominee to appear, was encouraged by the Dukakis campaign workers to call out "We want Mike!" at every pause. The speech, scheduled for fifteen minutes, took thirty-three to deliver, and Bill had to stop several times to ask for quiet, and was applauded only when he said the words, "in conclusion."

Bill pauses during his speech at the 1988 Democratic National Convention. *(Courtesy of AP Images)*

The speech, captured on nationwide television, made Bill the laughingstock of the nation. The *Washington Post* story about the speech was entitled "The Numb and the Restless," and several journalists said Bill had destroyed his career. The late-night talk show host Johnny Carson began making Bill the butt of many of his jokes.

Hillary knew something had to be done quickly. Bill, shocked by the negative reaction, was unsure how to respond. Hillary, however, jumped into action. She called her friends Harry Thomason and his wife Linda Bloodworth-Thomason, Arkansas natives who worked in Hollywood as producers of two popular comedy shows then running on television, *Designing Women* and *Evening Shade*. Together they devised a strategy. Because Johnny Carson was, at the time, the top late-night talk show host and had already made several jokes about the speech, Hillary and her two friends convinced Bill that he should appear on the show. The producers of the *Tonight Show* agreed for Bill to appear if he would play his saxophone with the band.

It was a risky maneuver, however. Johnny Carson's sharp wit was legendary, and if Bill's appearance was not a success, the damage to his public image would be devastating. But Hillary finally convinced him it was the only way to salvage his reputation.

The night of Bill's appearance, Carson delivered a long and rambling introduction that included trivia about Arkansas and Bill's personal biography. It was a hilarious parody of Bill's speech at the Democratic Convention and the audience roared with laughter. They clearly expected Johnny to have an easy time making jokes at the relatively unknown politician's expense.

But when Johnny finally finished his introduction, Bill entered the set laughing, and continued laughing at Johnny's pokes at him. He showed such good humor that Johnny seemed to enjoy his visit. Bill finished his appearance by playing the saxophone with the band, and when he left the stage, Johnny praised him for his sense of humor, and admitted he would have to find a new target for his jokes.

The national media covered Bill's appearance with Carson. There was general agreement that he had won over his critics with his ability to joke about himself. He had saved his political career—and Hillary was chiefly responsible for mapping out the successful strategy.

After the 1988 presidential campaign was over, and George H. W. Bush had overwhelmingly defeated Michael Dukakis, Hillary was appointed to a special committee, established by the American Bar Association, to investigate ways to end racially segregated schools. She also served as national chairperson of the Children's Defense Fund.

Also in 1988, the *National Law Journal*, the leading national publication for lawyers, named Hillary as one of the "100 Most Influential Lawyers In America." She was again named to the list in 1990. Clearly, Hillary had reached the top of the legal profession.

In 1990, Bill was selected as co-chair of a presidential summit on education held at the University of Virginia. The meeting of the nation's governors was a great success, and President Bush thanked him publicly for his help. Hillary attended the summit with Bill, and made a strong impression on President Bush when she pointed out to him that the United States was ranked seventeenth in the world in the rate of infant mortality, which is the number of babies that die before their first birthday.

Bush said she had to be wrong, but promised to check her statistics. The next day the president sent her a note through Bill admitting she was right.

During his 1990 reelection campaign for governor, Bill faced stiff opposition in the Democratic primary. One opponent was Tom McRae, and in the middle of the primary campaign, when Bill was away from Arkansas, McRae held a news conference and charged Bill with neglecting the state's needs.

Much to McRae's surprise, Hillary was in the audience. Angry at what she perceived as groundless charges against Bill's record, made when he was not present to defend himself, she challenged McRae.

When the stunned McRae repeated his charge that Bill was more interested in his national political ambitions than in serving as Arkansas's governor, Hillary pulled out a report issued by the Winthrop Rockefeller Foundation, a public policy group, which praised Bill's effort to improve the state. Reading from the report, she paused dramatically before reading the name of the chairman of the foundation when the report was issued—Tom McRae. Then she pressed McRae to reveal why he was criticizing Bill when he had previously praised him. McRae grew increasingly flustered and left the stage as soon as possible.

Hillary's actions at this press conference became a hot topic of discussion around the state. While some newspaper columnists, and some political opponents, accused her of being pushy, others admired her determination.

Bill won reelection in 1990, but the campaign was filled with many of the same personal charges against Bill and Hillary that would reappear in the 1992 presidential campaign, including charges that Bill engaged in repeated extramarital sexual affairs. There were also claims that the Rose Law Firm benefited unethically from Hillary's position as Arkansas's First Lady. Hillary thought the national Republican Party, afraid that Bill would be a formidable candidate if he ran for president in 1992, wanted to destroy his reputation. Chelsea was now old enough to understand, and to be hurt, by the political attacks on her parents. Hillary had to explain to her daughter that politics is often unpleasant.

After winning reelection, Bill announced it would be his last term as governor. It was time to move on toward national office or retire from politics and take up the practice of law. Both United States senators from Arkansas were Democrats and longtime friends of the Clintons. Bill could not challenge them by running for the U.S. Senate. His only alternative was to run for the presidency in 1992.

Hillary did not think it was realistic that Bill would be elected president in 1992. In 1991, a U.S.-lead coalition of troops, under the auspices of the United Nations, forced Iraqi dictator Saddam Hussein's army out of Kuwait. Saddam had invaded on the pretext that Kuwait was actually part of Iraq, but it was obvious he wanted to control even more of the oil reserves in the Middle East. After the successful Gulf War, President Bush's popularity in opinion polls rose to record levels. Most of the presumed Democratic candidates, including Senator Al Gore of Tennessee and Senator Bill Bradley of New Jersey, announced they would not run for president in 1992. They apparently thought it would be a waste of time to run against President Bush that year and decided to wait until 1996, when Bush could not run for reelection.

Bill, however, thought President Bush was neglecting many of the serious problems facing the country. The economy was not growing, health care costs were rising, and education reform was stalled nationwide. Many of the same problems Bill and Hillary had faced in Arkansas also plagued the nation, and Bill believed the country needed a president who would focus on the country's domestic problems. He sensed many Americans shared his concern over the direction the country was taking. But to run for president was an awesome task. Both Hillary and Bill knew the campaign would be long and difficult. Chelsea would be exposed to the same type of personal attacks experienced in the 1990 gubernatorial campaign, only this time the charges would be made on a national stage.

The other major candidates running for the Democratic nomination in 1992 were former Governor Jerry Brown of California, Senators Bob Kerrey of Nebraska and Tom Harkin of Iowa, former Massachusetts senator Paul Tsongas, and Virginia governor Douglas Wilder. Bill quickly emerged as the front-runner, as commentators, and early primary voters, were impressed by his understanding of the issues, and

Pictured here are the candidates who ran for the 1992 Democratic nomination: (from left) Bob Kerrey, Tom Harkin, Jerry Brown, Bill Clinton, and Paul Tsongas. *(Courtesy of AP Images/Jim Cole)*

his ability to make voters feel he was speaking directly to their concerns.

The New Hampshire primary was the first big test. Because the state is small it allowed Bill to present himself personally to many of the voters. Most people who met him were impressed by his intelligence and determination to win. However, Paul Tsongas, from neighboring Massachusetts, had an advantage in New Hampshire.

Hillary campaigned as hard as Bill. She spoke to all types of groups, not limiting herself to the more traditional women's groups as had previous candidates' wives. Hillary was as impressive as her husband, and articles began appearing about the Bill-Hillary team.

Then the Clinton campaign pollsters saw trouble in their surveys. Many poll respondents expressed misgivings about Hillary's role in the campaign. Although other politicians' wives have been crucial to their husbands' success, a high percentage of the poll respondents felt Hillary's position as chief strategist was inappropriate. Others thought she neglected her family because of personal ambitions. In many ways, these were the same public perceptions that had troubled her in Arkansas. Campaign advisors suggested she take a less public profile while they determined the best way to deal with the voter's negative impression of her.

Hillary was depressed by the poll results. She was a devoted mother and had committed a large portion of her career, usually without pay, toward improving children's lives. She had even traveled to France to research ways to more efficiently provide day care, health services, and education to needy children. And, most importantly, she had raised her daughter with love and had fought to hold her family together when she and Bill suffered marital problems. Although she realized political perceptions often were grounded more in image than in fact, to be perceived as a woman who cared little for "family values" hurt her deeply. However, she accepted the pollsters' suggestion and reduced her public appearances.

Then, before the Clinton campaign could work out a strategy to deal with Hillary's image problem, the world caved in on the campaign—and Hillary had no choice but to play a public role. In January 1992 a supermarket tabloid ran an article alleging Bill had had a long-term affair with a woman from Arkansas. The woman had previously denied similar rumors, but in the article she said she had been his mistress for ten years. When the national media picked up the story, Bill's campaign was severely damaged.

Some advisors in Bill's campaign suggested he drop out of the race. But Hillary, much as she had after the 1988 Democratic Convention fiasco, moved into action. She insisted they publicly attack the story. When the popular CBS news show *60 Minutes* offered them the opportunity to appear together and discuss the allegations, they accepted.

The interview aired on January 26, after the Super Bowl. In response to the questions by interviewer Steve Kroft, Bill denied he had ever had an affair with Gennifer Flowers. While admitting he had made mistakes during his marriage, he refused to reveal any more of his personal life.

Hillary turned out to be the focus of the newscast. Her eyes often flashed with barely repressed anger as she refuted the story. "You know," she told Kroft, "I'm not sitting here, some little woman standing by my man like Tammy Wynette."

The remark upset Wynette, and Hillary apologized. Nonetheless, Hillary's steely appearance was impressive, and it stopped Bill's slide in the polls. Her public display of devotion had helped save him from being driven from the race. However, questions and investigations of Bill's sex life would continue over the next years and eventually put his presidency at risk.

Although she helped the campaign overcome the tabloid allegations, Hillary did make mistakes. For example, later in the year, while she was visiting her hometown of Chicago, a reporter asked her about recent accusations made against her by Jerry Brown, who had criticized her work at Rose Law Firm and charged that, as governor, Bill had "funneled" money to the firm. These were old charges and Hillary denied them.

Hillary took an active role in Bill's 1992 campaign, and her public display of devotion to him helped bolster his campaign after he was accused of committing adultery. *(Courtesy of AP Images/Nick Ut)*

Then she added that she was being criticized because of her successful career, and said: "I suppose I could have stayed home and baked cookies and had teas. But what I decided to do was pursue my profession, which I entered before my husband was in public life."

The so-called "cookies and teas" line became an issue. Media stories began appearing about the Clinton campaign's "Hillary Problem." Reporters interviewed women who did not work outside the home, and reported that many of them were hurt and insulted by the comment. Even after Hillary apologized, the controversy continued.

Bill had plenty of other worries, including charges that he had avoided the draft during the Vietnam War. However, he persisted and eventually won enough votes to win the

Democratic presidential nomination. In the spring of 1992, however, most political pundits gave him little chance of winning in November. There were convinced he was damaged beyond repair. The race seemed to be between Ross Perot, a Texas billionaire who had entered the race as an independent and generated quite a bit of grassroots support, and President Bush.

Polls indicated that Hillary's image was more of a problem than ever. She had to do something to change people's impressions of her. She chose a familiar stage to begin redefining her image—a commencement address at Wellesley.

In this speech, Hillary revealed her deepest concerns and beliefs. Women should have the opportunity to choose their own path in life and should not be criticized for working inside the home any more than they should be criticized for pursuing public careers. And she let it be known that in both her public and private life, her primary concern was for children. The speech received extensive national coverage and began a reevaluation of Hillary by many voters.

During June, some leaders in the Democratic Party suggested publicly that Bill was so damaged by the tough primary campaign that he should be denied the nomination. They wanted the National Convention, to be held in July in New York City, to select a different candidate. This would turn out to be the low point of the campaign.

When Bill selected Al Gore, a popular senator, as his vice-presidential running mate, his standing in the polls began to improve, although the attention of the media, and of President Bush, was focused on Ross Perot, who had stunned the nation by shooting to the top of most major polls. Then, during the Democratic Convention, Ross Perot surprised the

Hillary jokes with vice presidential candidate Al Gore and his wife, Tipper, on their campaign tour bus. *(Courtesy of AP Images/Stephan Savoia)*

country again by suddenly announcing he was dropping out of the race. Almost overnight, Bill's poll ratings moved up nearly thirty points. The Bush campaign, all its attention now focused on Bill, renewed its efforts to portray Hillary as an enemy of the family. Quotes from the articles on children's rights she had written in the 1970s were used to accuse her of comparing marriage to slavery, and of encouraging children to sue their parents to get out of doing chores. During the Republican Convention, in August 1992, Pat Buchanan, a former presidential candidate, said Hillary was the enemy of everything traditional in American life.

Hillary's long days campaigning were made more pleasant when she met Tipper Gore, the wife of Al Gore. Tipper and

Hillary became close. However, Hillary did feel the need to return to Arkansas whenever possible to rest and see her daughter when she returned to school that fall. She tried to protect Chelsea from press attention by refusing requests for interviews and by guarding against unauthorized photographs.

First Lady Hillary Clinton *(Library of Congress)*

As the campaign moved into its final weeks, Bill's standing in the polls began to improve. Many voters were unhappy with the way the Republican Convention had focused so much attention on her and wanted the campaign to be fought over economic issues.

Although Ross Perot reentered the race in October and participated in the three national debates, Bill maintained his lead throughout the fall. On November 3, 1992, Bill Clinton was elected the forty-second president of the United States. Hillary Rodham Clinton was going to be the First Lady, the most prominent political woman in the nation.

nine
Managed Competition

Days after the election, media reports out of Little Rock, where Bill and his advisors were creating a new administration, began emphasizing Hillary's influence and questioning if the American public would accept an activist First Lady.

Even before Bill was inaugurated, controversy surrounded the Clinton family. Chelsea was the first school-age child to live in the White House since Amy Carter in the late 1970s. The Clintons were strong supporters of public schools, and Chelsea had attended city schools in Little Rock. But Hillary and Bill decided she should attend Sidwell Friends School, a private Quaker academy, when they moved to Washington. Their decision was determined by what they thought was best for Chelsea, who faced a tough transition to a new environment. But the choice angered many who thought Hillary and Bill were being hypocritical for removing Chelsea from public school.

The old problem of Hillary's dress continued to hound her when her choice of clothes for the inauguration was widely criticized by fashion designers and style critics. Her bright blue coat with matching blue velour, wide-brimmed hat was attacked for not being glamorous enough.

However, clothes had never been Hillary's primary concern, and after Bill was sworn in she reverted to practical, professional dress. That her mind was on more important things became evident when it was announced she would have a large office in the West Wing of the White House, where the most important members of the presidential staff have offices. Traditionally, the First Lady's office has been in the East Wing.

Bill hugs Hillary and Chelsea during his inauguration. *(Courtesy of AP Images/Amy Sancetta)*

Hillary would need the large office. Health care reform was one of the most hotly debated issues of the campaign and promised to be a contentious issue for the Clinton presidency.

Bill and Hillary agreed that the country's economic problems and long-term success would require that health care costs be brought under control and that all Americans have access to affordable health care. It was estimated in 1993 that more than 30 million Americans did not have health insurance.

On January 25, 1993, only five days after he took office, President Clinton announced the creation of the Task Force on National Health Care Reform, and that Hillary would be heading it up. The announcement took place in the Roosevelt Room, located in the West Wing of the White House. Bill promised the assembled journalists and other officials that the task force would present a comprehensive plan to reform health care to the U.S. Congress in one hundred days.

Hillary's top aide on the Health Care Task Force would be another old friend, Ira Magaziner. Magaziner graduated from Brown University the same year Hillary graduated from Wellesley, also spoke at his commencement, and was featured in the same *Life* magazine article as Hillary. Later, Magaziner, also a Rhodes Scholar, met Bill at Oxford.

There was a great deal of concern at the time—as there still is today—about the state of health care in the U.S. In 1993 more than 20 percent of the U.S. population had no health coverage. Most of those who did were covered through their job, which meant a layoff or job switch could leave them uncovered. If the employer decided to no longer cover the employees they would also be uninsured. Most worrisome, many of the most vulnerable citizens received inadequate care.

Inadequate coverage was not the only problem. The U.S. spends much more on health care than any other country. Bill and Hillary, and many economists, thought this was an unsustainable drain on the economy.

Trying to alter such an important part of people's lives, and the economy, was a monumental challenge. Presidents as far back as Franklin Roosevelt in the 1930s had talked about reforming the massive health care system. President Truman had proposed the creation of a system that would cover all Americans in 1948. Those efforts had failed. President Lyndon Johnson had convinced Congress to create two programs that expanded health care coverage. Medicare insures that senior citizens—those over sixty-five—have access to care. Medicaid attempted to provide coverage to the poor.

The most powerful opponents of health care reform were the insurance companies, pharmaceutical companies, and doctor's associations. All three groups feared that reform would hurt their businesses, and all three had vast resources that could be used to influence members of congress and the American people.

In the past, many of the ideas presented to reform health care were centered on what came to be called single-payer plans. In these schemes, all care would be funded by the taxpayers and operated out of governmental agencies, or another agency closely regulated by the federal government. The advocates of single-payer argued that it would be the best way to control costs and guarantee coverage. Opponents said it would lower the quality of coverage and lead to long waiting lists and fewer improvements in equipment and training.

Early on, Hillary and Magaziner decided to try another approach. They called their plan managed competition. Broadly speaking, managed competition tried to combine the best aspects of the current private system with the single-payer plans that were used in many other countries, including Canada and Great Britain. Instead of creating a system with strong governmental control, they envisioned a combination of private insurance companies, hospitals, and doctors, working within a network of laws and regulations designed to increase competition in order to control costs. Everyone would be covered and insurance companies would compete for business, constrained by the regulations. A set fee would be established for specific procedures, and the companies and hospitals would be motivated to find a way to deliver it for reduced costs. All employers, except for the smallest, would have to provide coverage, but there would be tax breaks and other incentives to make it more affordable.

A weakness of a managed competition plan was its complexity, a result of having to set fees for thousands of different services. This complexity left it open to a limitless number of criticisms by its opponents.

In his State of the Union address, delivered on January 25, 1994, President Clinton announced that he had no intention of compromising on their plan to reform health care. The Congress would either have to pass the entire package or reject it. He and Hillary argued that if parts were changed or taken out, or additions made, the entire plan would collapse. Their strategy was to pressure the Democrats in Congress to unify behind the plan and to quickly pass the bill. They knew that the longer it was delayed the more time those

Hillary holds a copy of the Clinton health care plan as she campaigns for its implementation. *(Courtesy of AP Images/Joe Marquette)*

opposed to its passing would be able to undercut its support with voters.

However, it soon became clear that they would have trouble holding even Democratic support. The biggest blow came when influential New York Democratic senator Daniel Patrick Moynihan—whose seat Hillary would win in 2000—predicted on a Sunday morning news show that the plan had little chance of passing.

As Bill and Hillary had predicted, the delay in winning congressional support also gave the insurance companies and other opponents time to organize and produce television commercials that claimed the plan would destroy health care in the United States. The most effective ad they produced had a husband and wife who were unable to decipher what the plan meant for them. The campaign was well produced and soon began to sway public opinion.

The final end of the attempt to reform health care came in the summer of 1994. The Democratic majority leader of the Senate advised the president and Hillary to try to find a way to compromise in order to pass at least part of their plan. But it was too late. Their refusal to compromise earlier now meant there were few people left in Congress who wanted to work with them. The commercials, designed to frighten the voters into not wanting any change in health care, had worked.

The collapse of her health care initiative was a bitter blow to Hillary and Bill. But a bigger political setback was on the horizon.

Health care had not been the only combustible issue Bill had addressed. The country faced massive budget deficits when he came to office. To combat this, he pushed a bill through Congress that raised taxes on the wealthiest taxpayers. Although the vast majority of citizens were not affected by the tax increases, passage of the bill left him vulnerable to political attacks.

As the 1994 midterm elections approached, Bill and Hillary faced a situation similar to what they had faced in Arkansas in 1980. They had again come into a new office full of ideals and dreams. At first it seemed that the majority of people were in support of his ideas, but over the following months that support had deteriorated.

Bill and Hillary expected their party would suffer some defeats in 1994, but had no idea how devastating it would be. When the votes were counted on election night the Democrats had lost eight senate seats and fifty-four seats in the U.S. House of Representatives. They were now the minority party in both houses. It was a debacle of historic proportions, one of the most dramatic political collapses in American history.

ten
First Lady

After the double setbacks of the failure of health care reform and the election losses, Hillary and Bill began to reevaluate their approach to the presidency. She scaled back her public role as a policy maker. The fight over health care reform had made her even more controversial than before. There was evidence that many voters were uncomfortable with a First Lady playing such a prominent role.

Although she would not again be in charge of initiatives, Hillary did not stop being a vital part of the Clinton administration. The leaders of the White House staff realized that the president listened to her more than anyone else. If they wanted to convince Bill to go along with their suggestions it was necessary to have Hillary's support.

Although she had stepped back from her public role, Hillary was still in the public eye—usually not by her choice. There had been charges made against her during the campaign over a land development deal on the Whitewater River that she and

Bill had lost money in as investors. This was only the first of a stream of accusations of unethical conduct made throughout the eight years she was First Lady. Most of the charges concerned, in some way, her work at Rose Law Firm, and were investigated by the independent counsel office. She was never charged with any crime or found to be guilty of any illegal or unethical behavior, but the political controversy took a constant toll.

Kenneth Starr *(Courtesy of AP Images/ Dennis Cook)*

In August 1994, Bill agreed to ask a panel made up of three judges, two of which were appointed by Republicans, to appoint Kenneth Starr, a former lawyer in the Bush administration, to investigate the failed Whitewater development. After the Republican victories in November 1994, the Whitewater investigation morphed into a confusing assortment of charges involving the Rose Law Firm, other politicians in Arkansas, a failed savings and loan, as well as Bill and Hillary's personal lives. The investigations would continue throughout the remainder of the Clinton administration.

Meanwhile, Bill and Hillary tried to forge ahead as president and First Lady, which became more difficult after the 1994 elections.

In Washington the years 1995 and 1996 were character-ized by an ongoing tension between Bill and the Republican Congress. The biggest conflict was over how the U.S. gov-ernment would collect and spend taxes. The budget conflict finally culminated in a government shutdown that began on November 13, 1995, when Bill refused to accept the budget presented by the Republicans. He argued that the Republican

The federal office building in Oklahoma City after it was bombed by an anti-government terrorist *(Courtesy of the Department of Defense)*

budget would seriously hurt the poorest people in the country, as well as undercut many of the programs necessary for future growth. When the negotiations collapsed, there was no alternative but to close all nonessential government services and to send thousands of federal workers home. In political terms the shutdown was a high-wire act between the administration and Congress. It was soon obvious that the administration was winning. Polls indicated that most people blamed the Republicans in Congress for the shutdown and a compromise was worked that blocked most of the cuts Bill had resisted.

Months before the government shutdown, terrorists led by Timothy McVeigh had set off a truck bomb in front of a federal office building in Oklahoma City, Oklahoma. One hundred and sixty-eight people died in the attack, which occurred on April 19, 1995. Bill and Hillary traveled to the memorial service and he spoke to the survivors and grieving family. It was one of the most tragic events in American history and riveted the country's attention.

By the 1996 election campaign, the economy was strong and the popularity of Congress had declined. Weeks before the election Bill had signed a welfare reform bill that was widely popular. The Republicans nominated Senate Majority Leader Robert Dole, who had run for president twice before. But Dole was never able to get traction with the voters, and Bill won easily.

The second term of the Clinton administration seemed to hold out promise. There was the chance for a new era of cooperation between Democrats and Republicans. But before long the acrimony returned.

Kenneth Starr had continued his investigations, eventually shifting most of the focus from a search for financial irregularities to investigate rumors of Bill's extramarital affairs. After a magazine published an article claiming Bill had had sex with a state employee while he was governor, the woman mentioned in the article, Paula Jones, had sued Bill and accused him of sexual harassment. As the civil suit, funded by an organization committed to ending the Clinton presidency, gradually worked through the courts, Jones's lawyers began working closely with the Starr investigators. In January 1998, they were finally able to go public with a charge against Bill they were able to prove.

Hillary writes in her memoir that on the morning of January 21, Bill woke her to tell her that the newspapers were reporting that he had had a sexual relationship with a young presidential intern named Monica Lewinsky. Furthermore, it was reported that he had lied and denied the affair while under oath.

Almost immediately the Clintons' political opponents began demanding that Bill resign. If he refused to resign they promised to impeach him.

The controversy continued for months. Initially, Bill denied publicly and to Hillary that the stories were true, and that he had not lied under oath. On August 17, 1998, he had to testify before a grand jury. This time he admitted to what he called an inappropriate relationship with Monica Lewinsky. It soon became apparent that the Starr investigators had more proof of the affair, and the calls for Bill's impeachment intensified.

Eventually, as had the other disputes between Bill and his opponents, the scandal boiled down to which side people supported. Most of Bill's supporters, and a majority of Americans, came to accept that he had engaged in adultery

Even after Bill admitted to having an inappropriate relationship with Monica Lewinsky, Hillary still supported him publicly. *(Courtesy of AP Images/Marty Lederhandler)*

and had not been honest about it. However, they felt that impeachment and removing a president from office should be reserved for crimes such as corruption, treason, or other crimes that materially hurt the state, not lying about adultery. Supporters of impeachment argued that regardless of what he lied about, the president had committed perjury and should be removed from office, and that he had committed immoral behavior.

The polls indicated that most Americans did not want the president to be impeached. But the years of conflict had created too deep a reservoir of distrust and anger. Although they suffered defeats in the 1998 midterm elections, the Republican leaders of the house voted to impeach Bill. After the house voted to impeach, it was the Senate's duty to try the crimes, as in a court of law, and vote on the question of whether Bill should be removed from office. The final vote came far short of the two-thirds majority needed to remove the president.

Throughout the public ordeal, Hillary had to deal with her husband's adultery and dishonesty about it in the glare of political and media attention. She was torn between supporting her husband in a political fight with their long-term enemies and deciding if she would divorce Bill. She decided to support Bill publicly, which helped to swing public opinion in his favor. But she had a harder time deciding to forgive him and to remain married, which was her eventual decision.

After the impeachment drama, Bill still had two years in office. Remarkably, his popularity increased. The economy was strong and the series of investigations had finally run out of energy. He focused on trying to forge peace between the Palestinian Arabs and Israel, and trying to capture or kill terrorist leader Osama bin Laden. He also continued to work for peace in the war-torn former Yugoslavia.

Bill loved being president. His last two years were bittersweet because he and Hillary both knew it would end soon. But the end of Bill's presidency did not mean the Clinton family was finished with politics.

eleven
New State

On February 12, 1999, the same day the Senate met to vote on the articles of impeachment, Hillary met with longtime friend and aide Harold Ickes, a veteran of New York state politics. Senator Daniel Patrick Moynihan had recently announced he would not run for reelection in 2000. Soon after Moynihan's announcement, political pundits and friends of Hillary began to publicly and privately promote her as a possible candidate. Initially, Hillary publicly tried to laugh off the speculation. No First Lady had ever run for political office.

The fact that Hillary had never lived in New York was not a roadblock if she decided to run. Others had moved to New York to run for statewide office. In 1964, after he resigned as U.S. attorney general, Robert Kennedy moved to New York and ran for the U.S. Senate and won easily. Of all the fifty states, New York might have been the most receptive to Hillary as their senator.

There were other obstacles, however. Hillary was one of the most polarizing figures in the country. Enemies of the Clintons had accused her of a wide variety of criminal and immoral deeds. Although none of the charges had been proven, the relentless campaign against her had inevitably damaged her reputation.

Ironically, the Lewinsky scandal might have enhanced Hillary's chances. After Bill publicly admitted to the affair and that he had lied to Hillary about it, there was an outpouring of public sympathy for her. She was visibly hurt by his deceit and even many of her enemies felt that she was also a victim in the affair. However, Hillary and her advisors knew that if she entered the race much of that sympathy would dry up. Once she became a viable candidate they would unleash more of the furious opposition she and Bill had experienced in the past.

Early on in her deliberations it became clear that Hillary faced other challenges in New York. The Democratic Party in the state let her know that if she chose to run, the leadership would work to keep anyone from challenging her in the primary. But as it became more likely she would run, the state Republicans began a nationwide fund raising campaign. Their argument was that Republicans everywhere needed to come together to stop Hillary.

New York Republicans consolidated behind the candidacy of Rudy Giuliani, the mayor of New York City. Similar to Hillary, Giuliani was controversial. Many African Americans in the city accused him of caring little for their interests. He had consistently backed the New York City police in cases when African American leaders insisted the police had used unjust force. But Giuliani could also claim that he had cut

Hillary's Republican opponent in the 2000 Senate race was New York Mayor Rudy Giuliani. *(Courtesy of AP Images/Don Heupel)*

the crime rate in the nation's largest city and that he had improved its reputation.

Although many of Hillary's closest friends and advisors recommended that she not run, Hillary decided in late May of 1999 that she was going to make the attempt. Harold Ickes, who would be in charge of much of the campaign, later remembered that he picked up his ringing phone and heard Hillary say, "I'm doing this." She had no illusions about how hard it would be, but she knew that if she wanted to continue with her public service, winning a Senate seat in one of the most populous states would be a powerful political platform.

Because the Democratic Party in New York was aligned behind Hillary she was able to avoid a bruising fight for the nomination. Her support was so solid that even Senator

Moynihan, who had a strained relationship with the Clinton administration, allowed her to announce she was running from his farm. On July 1, 1999, Hillary, Senator Moynihan, and more than one hundred national, state, and local reporters gathered to hear Hillary promise to spend the next months listening to New Yorkers express their needs and concerns in order to learn what they expected from her as their senator.

The first phase of the campaign was dubbed the "Listening Tour." Instead of large arenas and public speeches, Hillary decided to travel the state and meet with small groups of citizens and with local reporters. At night, between stops, she studied local issues and soon had an impressive knowledge of the needs of the towns and cities throughout the state. Eventually, however, the listening tour began to be criticized. Reporters began to suggest Hillary was trying to avoid their tough questions.

Meanwhile, Mayor Giuliani was gathering large amounts of money and consolidating his party's support. He hoped that because he was so well known in New York City he would be able to devote most of his attention elsewhere in the state. He was sure his tough image would win him support in the more rural, conservative areas of the state.

But all was not smooth sailing for Giuliani. His zeal to reduce crime had earned him most of his positive reputation but had also alienated those who lived in the poorer neighborhoods. Also, Giuliani had won the mayor's office in 1993 by defeating David Dinkins, the city's first African American mayor.

As the Senate campaign was heating up, Giuliani suddenly faced another crisis involving race. On the early morning hours of March 16, 2000, an African American man named Patrick Dorismond was shot and killed by two undercover narcotics officers. There was no evidence that Dorismond possessed drugs at the time of the shooting. When the police officers came under intense criticism, and there were calls that they be arrested and tried for killing a man who was not committing a crime, Giuliani had the city's lawyer release Dorismond's juvenile police records, which are usually kept sealed. This set off an enraged reaction; it appeared that the mayor, in his zeal to protect the police, was sullying a dead man's reputation.

Even in the midst of the controversy around the Dorismond affair, Giuliani looked to many political observers to be the favorite over Hillary. One critical factor was fundraising. Hillary had become so controversial that in some conservative quarters she was probably hated, and feared, even more than Bill. This provided a deep reservoir of support for Giuliani. By January 2000 he had raised almost 30 million dollars; Hillary had less than 20 million. But soon a dramatic change would alter the 2000 race.

There had long been rumors that Giuliani and his second wife were on the verge of divorce. But when a newspaper reported that the mayor was romantically involved with another woman, and had been seen having dinner with her in a restaurant, there was another media storm. If there had not been so much publicity about the troubles in Hillary's marriage, and the long attempt to remove Bill from office because of the Lewinsky scandal, Giuliani's personal life might have been less of a story, but now the Republican candidate was open to charges of hypocrisy.

Almost simultaneously with the revelation of his marriage difficulties, Giuliani announced he had been diagnosed with prostate cancer. Initially, he said he did not know the cancer would affect his Senate race. Then, on May 19, 2000, the mayor announced that he was withdrawing from the race.

Within twenty-four hours after Giuliani's withdrawal, Rick Lazio, a U.S. representative from Long Island, announced he would run in the mayor's place. Lazio was young and attractive, and had been in Congress for eight years. Although he was not as well known as Giuliani, he was a formidable candidate. Within days he was tied with Hillary in most polls.

During the summer of 2000 and into the fall, however, most political observers agreed that Lazio made one fundamental mistake. Instead of spending more of his time and money introducing himself to voters and making his positions on issues clear, his commercials and speeches primarily attacked Hillary for not being a "real" New Yorker, and he said she was out-of-touch with most New Yorkers. This strategy did little to win over those who had not yet decided which candidate to support.

As the campaign entered its final weeks Hillary began to pull ahead. Her campaign had run several negative ads against Lazio but had mixed them up with more positive commercials and speeches that attempted to lay out what she thought were the biggest problems facing the state and what she proposed to do about the problems.

The climax of the campaign came in the first of three scheduled debates. During most of the debate it seemed that Lazio was holding his own, or even doing slightly better than Hillary. Then, in the last few minutes, he challenged Hillary

Lazio gives Hillary a pledge to limit campaign contributions and demands that she sign it during this debate. *(Courtesy of AP Images/Richard Drew)*

to sign a pledge to limit campaign contributions, which had become a major issue.

In the heat of the exchange Lazio pulled a sheet of paper from his pocket that he said was a pledge he was willing to sign if Hillary signed also. When she said that first she would have to read it, Lazio crossed the stage and, standing only inches from Hillary, began to wave the paper and said, "Right here, sign it, right now!" Hillary refused.

Lazio thought his tactic was effective, but soon polls revealed that many voters, even those unsympathetic to Hillary, responded negatively to what they saw as his threatening, heavy-handed tactic. Many women in particular were upset that he had moved so close to Hillary, and the airwaves and newspapers were filled with talk of how he had "invaded her personal space."

The campaign still had several weeks to go, and Lazio continued to campaign and run hard-hitting commercials, but he was never able to recover. Hillary was not a charismatic politician, particularly when compared to Bill, and had come into the state facing powerful opposition and a skeptical public. But the chaos on the Republican side, as well as their refusal to address her directly on the issues, had probably been a mistake. On election day, Hillary won by a margin of 55 to 43 percent, a landslide by New York standards.

Now it was time to return to Washington, D.C., this time as a leader in her own right. She had no way of knowing that only months after she was sworn into office her state, and the entire nation, would face one of the gravest challenges in its history.

twelve
Senator Clinton

W hen Hillary Clinton took the oath and became New York's junior senator in January 2001, her primary goal was to avoid the conflict that had characterized so much of her years in the White House. The Democrats were still in a minority, and if she wanted to be in a position to help her constituents she needed to work with her former opponents. The best way to do this was to avoid media attention as much as possible and to prove she was serious about being a productive senator.

Most of the senate's work is done in committees. Hillary was appointed to the Armed Services Committee, which oversees military spending and readiness. She was also appointed to the Committee on Health, Education, Labor, and Pensions, as well as Environment and Public Works and the Special Committee on Aging. She was also appointed to some subcommittees.

Her priorities as a senator from New York changed dramatically on September 11, 2001, when two planes flew into

After the 9/11 terrorist attacks, Hillary worked to make sure New York received the help it needed to recover. *(Courtesy of FEMA)*

the twin towers of the World Trade Center in lower New York City. The terrorist attack brought down the buildings and killed over three thousand citizens, including dozens of New York City firemen who were working to rescue people when the buildings collapsed. The terrorists also flew a plane into the Pentagon building outside of Washington, D.C. Another plane crashed in Pennsylvania.

After the disaster, Hillary set out to make sure her new state got the help it needed to recover, and to push for better homeland security. She helped to have money appropriated to rebuild the World Trade Center site and to compensate the victims of the attacks.

When President George W. Bush announced that he was sending U.S. troops into Afghanistan to overthrow the Taliban government that had supported and protected the terrorists, she promised her full support. Although she was bitterly disappointed that Osama bin Laden, the leader of al-Qaeda, the band of radical Islamic terrorists who had carried out the attacks, escaped capture, she said it was important to remove the Taliban from power.

Soon after the terrorist attacks President Bush began pushing to invade the nation of Iraq, which he said possessed chemical, biological, and maybe even nuclear weapons. He also insisted that Iraq's dictator, Saddam Hussein, supported terrorists and might have even been secretly involved in the September 11, 2001, terrorists' attacks. When the Senate voted on giving the president permission to invade Iraq, Hillary spoke in favor of the resolution and voted for it. She felt that any president should have the ability to perform the duties of commander-in-chief. She also was convinced by the evidence presented by several members of the Bush administration, including the director of the Central Intelligence Agency, that Saddam Hussein did possess dangerous weapons and should be stopped.

U.S. troops, assisted by a small number of soldiers from a few other nations, including Great Britain, invaded Iraq in March 2003. Although the official Iraqi army was quickly defeated, and Saddam Hussein was eventually captured and executed, the military situation in Iraq soon deteriorated. A combination of anti-American terrorists from other Islamic nations and insurgent groups in Iraq who resented the invasion began making guerrilla attacks against U.S. troops. American soldiers were being killed in increasing numbers by hidden explosives, suicide bombers, and sniper attacks.

Complicating the situation in Iraq were the religious divisions in the country. The two main branches of Islam, Sunni and Shia, had been rivals for centuries. Once the oppressive

American troops attend a training exercise in Iraq. Although Hillary initially voted for the resolution to invade Iraq, she became increasingly opposed to ongoing war there. *(Courtesy of the Department of Defense)*

control of Saddam Hussein was gone, the tensions between the two groups became more pronounced. Soon U.S. troops were caught between various terrorist groups who resented the invasion, as well as a bloody religious conflict between the Sunni and Shia.

Hillary, along with many others, was disappointed when no weapons of mass destruction were found in Iraq. The main rationale for the war that had been presented by President Bush was that Saddam Hussein possessed stockpiles of weapons that could be used in terrorist attacks against the U.S. and its allies. However, after extensive searches, no weapons were found. Eventually, President Bush said he had received faulty intelligence reports, but there was suspicion that the threat had been exaggerated in order to convince members of Congress, as well as the American people, to support the invasion. Hillary eventually regretted voting for the war resolution, but refused to say it was a mistake. She insisted she had made her decision on the evidence presented to the Congress, which turned out to be incorrect.

During the 2004 campaign, the Democrats nominated Senator John Kerry from Massachusetts to run against President Bush. Hillary campaigned for Kerry and criticized the president for how he had gained support for the invasion and for what she called his incompetent management of the conflict. Although the president was reelected, Hillary was enthusiastically received in most of the places she spoke.

Hillary faced reelection in 2006. In the two years leading up to the campaign she increasingly spoke out against the ongoing war in Iraq. However, she continued to refuse to say her vote for the war resolution was a mistake. Regardless, she was reelected in 2006 in a landslide.

Soon after the 2006 election Hillary faced a decision: should she run for president? Although she kept her thoughts private, most observers and her fellow members of congress expected her to run. As other Democrats and Republicans let it be known that they intended to run for president, pressure mounted to make a public announcement of her intentions.

Finally, on January 20, 2007, two years to the day before a new president would be inaugurated, Hillary posted the video in which she said she was going to begin her run for the highest office in the land on her Web site.

Still, Hillary faces some serious obstacles. In addition to facing the same hurdles any woman would have to surmount, she remains a divisive and controversial figure. The failed Republican attempts to force her husband out of the presidency, and her staunch support of him, still infuriate many.

Hillary stands between John Edwards (left) and Barack Obama (right) during a 2007 Democratic presidential debate. *(Courtesy of AP Images/ Charles Dharapak)*

Also, she lacks the charisma of some other politicians. Her vote for the Iraq war, and her refusal to apologize for it and to say it was a mistake, is criticized by a large segment of the Democratic Party.

However, no one, even her most determined enemies, can deny that Hillary Clinton is a fighter, who will not be easily defeated. In many ways, she is still the determined girl from Park Ridge who learned how to stand up to bullies. Her opponents underestimate her at their peril.

Timeline

1947   Born October 26 in Chicago.

1962   Travels with church group to Chicago to hear Dr. Martin Luther King Jr. speak; shakes Dr. King's hand; attends Maine Township East High School in Park Ridge, IL.

1965   Moves to Maine South High School for her senior year; organizes a campus wide teach-in about Vietnam War and participates in nationwide television show *College Bowl*; graduates from Maine South; starts at Wellesley College.

1968   Works as volunteer on Senator Eugene McCarthy's campaign for Democratic presidential nomination.

1969   Gives commencement speech at her graduation ceremony at Wellesley; enters Yale Law School.

1970   Works with Marian Wright Edelman during summer break.

1972   Travels to Texas to work for the campaign of George McGovern, the Democratic nominee for president.

1973   Receives J.D. from Yale Law School; moves to Cambridge, Massachusetts, to work with Marian Wright Edelman's new organization, the Children's Defense Fund.

1974   Leaves Children's Defense Fund to serve on staff of House Judiciary Committee, researching legal procedures, as part of the team investigating the Watergate scandal; after visiting Bill Clinton in Arkansas, accepts a teaching position at the University of Arkansas Law School.

1975 Marries Bill Clinton.

1976 Joins the Rose Law Firm; Bill Clinton elected attorney general of Arkansas.

1977 Appointed to the national board of directors of the Legal Services Corporation by President Jimmy Carter.

1978 Bill elected governor of Arkansas.

1980 Daughter Chelsea born; Bill defeated in reelection bid.

1982 Appointed chair of Arkansas Education Standards Committee by Bill Clinton, after he is elected governor a second time.

1988 Named one of the "100 Most Influential Lawyers in America" by the *National Law Journal*.

1991 Bill Clinton announces his run for president.

1992 Appointed to head the Task Force on National Health Care Reform by Bill Clinton, days after Clinton is elected the forty-second president of the United States.

1999 Decides to run for the U.S. Senate seat long held by New York senator Daniel Patrick Moynihan.

2000 Elected to U.S. Senate.

2006 Wins reelection to the Senate.

2007 Announces candidacy for U.S. president on January 20.

Sources

CHAPTER ONE: Park Ridge

p. 12, "There is no room . . . " Hillary Clinton, *Living History: Hillary Rodham Clinton* (New York: Simon & Shuster, 2003), 12.

CHAPTER TWO: Wellesley

p. 25, "I find myself . . . lots of sympathy," Hillary Clinton, "Hillary D. Rodham's Student Commencement Speech 1969," Wellesley College, press release, http://www.wellesley.edu/bpublicaffairs/commencement/1969/053169hillary.html.

CHAPTER FOUR: Young Lawyer

p. 40, "Why are you . . . with him," Sara Ehrman, "Stories of Bill," *Frontline Online*, http://www.pbs.org/wgbh/pages/frontline/shows/choice/bill/ehrman.html.

p. 43, "sweet-looking," Clinton, *Living History*, 74.

p. 43, "I bought it . . ." Ibid.

CHAPTER SIX: Ms. Clinton

p. 53, "Chelsea, this is new . . ." Clinton, *Living History*, 85.

p. 54, "I teared up . . ." Carl Bernstein, *A Woman In Charge: The Life of Hillary Rodham Clinton* (New York: Knopf, 2007), 166.

CHAPTER SEVEN: Arkansas Decade

p. 57, "guarantee that I will . . ." Donnie Radcliffe, *Hillary Rodham Clinton* (New York: Warner Books, 1993), 203.

p. 60, "Well, fellas, it looks . . ." Gail Sheehy, *Hillary's Choice* (New York: Ballantine, 1999), 153.

CHAPTER EIGHT: Campaign Issues

p. 73, "You know . . ." Clinton, *Living History*, 107.

p. 74, "I suppose I could . . ." Ibid., 109.

CHAPTER ELEVEN: New State

p. 94, "I'm doing this," Michael Tomasky, *Hillary's Turn: Inside Her Improbable Victorious Senate Campaign*, 49.

p. 98, "Right here, sign . . . " Ibid., 238.

Bibliography

Bernstein, Carl. *A Woman In Charge: The Life of Hillary Rodham Clinton.* New York: Knopf, 2007.

Bruck, Connie. "Hillary the Pol." *New Yorker,:* May 30, 1993.

Clinton, Bill. *My Life.* New York: Knopf, 2004.

Clinton, Hillary. *Living History.* New York: Simon & Schuster, 2003.

————. Hillary. *It Takes a Village.* New York: Simon & Schuster, 1996.

Dumas, Ernest. *The Clintons of Arkansas.* Fayetteville, Arkansas: University of Arkansas Press, 1993.

Harris, John. *The Survivor: Bill Clinton in the White House.* New York: Random House, 2005.

Klein, Joe. *The Natural: The Misunderstood Presidency of Bill Clinton.* New York: Doubleday, 2002.

Maraniss, David. *First In His Class: A Biography of Bill Clinton.* New York: Simon & Schuster, 1995.

Milton, Joyce. *The First Partner: Hillary Rodham Clinton.* New York: William Morrow and Company, 1999.

Radcliffe, Donnie. *Hillary Rodham Clinton.* New York: Warner Books, 1993.

Sheehy, Gail. *Hillary's Choice.* New York: Ballantine, 1999.

Tomasky, Michael. *Hillary's Turn: Inside Her Improbable Victorious Senate Campaign.* New York: The Free Press, 2001.

Warner, Judith. *Hillary Clinton: The Inside Story.* New York: New American Library, 1993.

Web sites

http://www.hillaryclinton.com
Hillary Clinton's official campaign Web site.

http://clinton.senate.gov
Hillary Clinton's Senate Web site. Among other things, it features links to a short biography.

http://topics.nytimes.com/top/reference/timestopics/people/c/hillary_rodham_clinton
This *New York Times* page on Hillary Rodham Clinton links to hundreds of pages of news articles, feature stories, and editorials written by *Times* reporters about Senator Clinton, dating back to 1992.

Index